T0143798

The
Mostly Mozart

Guide to
Mozart

The
Mostly Mozart
Guide to
Mozart

CARL VIGELAND

Introduction by Jane Moss
ARTISTIC DIRECTOR, MOSTLY MOZART FESTIVAL
and
Louis Langrée
RENÉE AND ROBERT BELFER MUSIC DIRECTOR
MOSTLY MOZART FESTIVAL

Lincoln Center

WILEY

John Wiley & Sons, Inc.

Library of Congress Cataloging-in-Publication Data:

Vigeland, Carl A.
   The Mostly Mozart guide to Mozart/Carl Vigeland; introduction by Jane Moss and Louis Langrée
      p. cm.
   Includes index.
   Includes discography.
   ISBN 978-0-470-19530-7 (cloth)
   ISBN 978-1-68442-703-1 (pbk)
      1. Mozart, Wolfgang Amadeus, 1756-1791—Criticism and interpretation.
      I. Mostly Mozart Festival.   II. Title.
ML410. M9V44 2009
780.92—dc22
[B]

                                                                  2009009728

From time to time the news that Mozart's skull has been identified causes a brief sensation, only for it to be discovered that it is not his after all. In any case the mortal remains and their whereabouts are not of great importance. What is important, perennially, is not the skull but what was inside it, which lives on in the minds and hearts of unnumbered thousands for whom it is a reason for being alive.

—David Cairns, author of *Mozart and His Operas*

CONTENTS

PREFACE   ix

ACKNOWLEDGMENTS   xiii

THE HISTORY OF THE
MOSTLY MOZART FESTIVAL   x v

INTRODUCTION
    by Jane Moss and Louis Langrée   1

PART ONE
    Mozart's Biography: A Hero's Life   5
    On the Road   10
    Home in Salzburg   14
    Vienna and the World   17
    Chronology   26

PART TWO
    Mozart's Works: Let There Be Music   29
    Symphonies and Orchestral Works   36
    Concertante   63

Contents

Concertos for Strings and Winds 71

Chamber Music 79

Vocal Music 87

Piano Music 106

Opera 139

CONCLUSION: MOZART AND MORTALITY 201

A PERSONAL NOTE 211

READING MOZART 215

NOTES TO PAGES XV–XXI 219

CREDITS 221

INDEX 223

PREFACE

Few composers in Western classical music have gen-
erated a greater wealth of commentary than Mozart,
in part because his vast creation was concentrated in
such a tragically brief life. As a consequence, a guide
to Mozart and his music must of necessity be selective,
rather than encyclopedic. In addition, because Mozart
was not only prolific but inventive beyond any degree
of ordinary imagining, an orderly division of his oeuvre
into neat, tidy categories runs the risk of missing his
foremost accomplishment: changing the way we listen
to music.

As you use this guide, therefore, keep in mind that
everything he did is related. To apprehend this fully might
demand the equivalent of a multidimensional musical
hologram.

In piece after piece, Mozart redefined the art in which
he composed, and the repercussions of that revolution

Created from a screen print by Robert Motherwell, this poster celebrated the 1991 Mostly Mozart Festival.

are with us still. He both built on what had come before him and left a legacy for other composers to learn from, be inspired by, and add to. That process continues today. To appropriate the phrase that sprang up spontaneously after the death of the jazz icon Charlie Parker, Mozart lives.

ACKNOWLEDGMENTS

Nurtured by my parents, Hans and Ruth Vigeland, both musicians, and by my godfather, the conductor Josef Krips, I began my formal Mozart education with several Mozart duets that my childhood piano teacher, Hazel McNamara, assigned to me when I was eight or nine years old. Haidie, as I called her, taught me an appreciation for Mozart's sense of form, his rhythmic and harmonic nuance, and his love of melody. Sitting with me at the piano bench in the home she shared with her sister and brother-in-law, she reached over with her right hand to correct fingerings and sang my part while I played. Decades later, when I am listening to a favorite Mozart concerto, I can still hear Haidie's voice and see her smile when I played something well. I owe her a debt of thanks that I can never repay.

My gratitude extends to my brother, Nils, a composer and pianist, who helped me here with questions of music theory and technique. I am also grateful to my wife,

Bonnie, who brought home books and recordings for me from the Hampshire College library. Thanks to the artists who mused on Mozart: Emanuel Ax, Sir James Galway, Rob Kapilow, James Levine, Amnon Levy, and Hao Jiang Tian and Lois Morris, who graciously allowed us to adapt a small portion of *Along the Roaring River: My Wild Ride from Mao to the Met*. Thanks also to Ann R. Maggs at the Amherst College music library, from which, despite tardiness with due dates and the disaster of a midsummer flood in my basement office, I was able to borrow scores and Mozartiana freely and frequently. Professor Norman Sims, the chair of the University of Massachusetts online journalism certificate program, for which I teach a course on writing about music, lent me his enthusiastic encouragement. Moral support came often in the form of e-mails and voice mails from friends, including Denis Laflamme, the founder of the Esselon Café in Hadley, Massachusetts, where I wrote parts of this book, and Larry Pruner, the proprietor of Valley Books. Thanks also to Gwen Briere, Wayne S. Kabak, Stanley J. Rabinowitz, Sandra J. Staub, and Christopher Vyce for advice, friendship, and counsel, and to the Corporation of Yaddo, where I revised my initial drafts during a month long residency. Finally, I wish to thank Jane Moss, artistic director of the Mostly Mozart Festival at Lincoln Center and, at John Wiley & Sons, production editor Rachel Meyers, freelance copy editor Patricia Waldygo, and my editor, Hana Lane. Hana first broached the subject of this volume over a sunny Manhattan breakfast and with great patience and tact guided me through the labyrinthine turns inevitably encountered by anyone lucky enough to be writing about Mozart. This is her book, too.

THE HISTORY OF THE MOSTLY MOZART FESTIVAL

> Mozart is the greatest composer of all . . . the
> music of Mozart is of such purity and beauty
> that one feels he merely "found it"—that it has
> always existed as part of the inner beauty of the
> universe waiting to be revealed.
>
> —Albert Einstein

One genius reflects on another, with the perspective of nearly two hundred years adding to the weight of Einstein's conclusion. Yet only fifteen years after Mozart's death in 1791, a court musician wrote: "He was a meteor on the musical horizon, for whose appearance we were not yet prepared."[1] Admired in his age and in ours, Mozart bequeathed to the ages musical riches in which everyone can delight.

Lincoln Center's air-conditioning—still a technological novelty in the late 1950s and early 1960s, but a welcome blessing in the sweltering humidity of a New York summer—presented both an opportunity and a challenge: how to fill the halls to best advantage programmatically and financially during the summer, when the resident companies were not performing. At that time, the "season" began in mid-September and ended in late May, creating the possibility that the plaza could become an urban desert and the halls a financial drain during June, July and August. Yet the Center's planners were motivated by more than just the need for additional revenue to keep its operations in the black. One of their primary mandates was to "encourage, sponsor or facilitate performances,"[2] and they intended to do exactly that.

Planning initially focused on Philharmonic Hall, which Schuyler Chapin, Lincoln Center's programming director at the time, once described as a "great big white elephant."[3] Early on, the Center took a gamble, producing a small concert series called August Fanfare in the summer of 1963. Management discovered that an audience for serious music during the summer did in fact exist,[4] and they began thinking about fashioning additional summer programming.

Midsummer Serenades: A Mozart Festival, as it was initially known, proved to be a brilliant collaboration among William Schuman; Chapin, Chapin's young assistant, William Lockwood; and two independent producers, Jay K. Hoffman and George F. Schutz. Midsummer Serenades, which opened in August 1966, featured the New York Chamber Orchestra, distinguished soloists, guest conductors and chamber music recitals. All tickets were $3, a bargain even then. The *New York Times* heralded the Mozart festival's debut this way: "Twenty-six Mozart programs are being given in Philharmonic Hall this month. If the prospect seems a little stupefying on first consideration, last night's opening concert provided the simple, clear answer:

You can't go wrong on Mozart. Provided, of course, you have a shrewdly arranged program, an ensemble of crack instrumentalists, a distinguished soloist and a sensitive conductor. All these were in evidence at the initial event, getting the series off to an excellent start."[5]

Mozart at reasonable prices was a winning formula. Audiences loved it, and the program's popularity convinced Schuman and Chapin that summer programming could generate revenue as well as fill an important programming need. "The lures were informality and affordability . . . And there was a come-as-you-are atmosphere in the early years that gave the series lively spirit."[6] Who had the original idea continues to be a matter of dispute, but the choice of Mozart seemed obvious: As Lockwood was quoted as saying, "He wrote enough music of enough variety to sustain such a survey."[7] By 1970, the festival, which already had added works by Haydn and Schubert, became known simply as Mostly Mozart, more accurately reflecting its offerings. Lockwood, who by that time had become the Center's director of programming, was the festival's director and in-house programmer.

Clever advertising campaign slogans during those first years captured the spirit of Mostly Mozart: "Savage Breasts Soothed Here"; "So Don't Put on a Tie"; and "As Much a Fixture of Summer as the Good Humor Man." They challenged New Yorkers and tourists alike: "What would summer be in New York without baseball, outdoor theater, street fairs and, of course, Mostly Mozart? Mostly hot, humid and humdrum. That's what."

What had begun as a four-week festival expanded gradually to five, then six, and finally in 1981 to seven weeks, because the previous seasons' concerts had been mostly standing room only. Yet the festival still had no permanent musical director, and its resident orchestra rotated with visiting chamber music groups. In 1982, to quell criticisms about the orchestra's inconsistency, Lincoln Center appointed Gerard Schwarz—who had debuted with Mostly Mozart as a trumpet soloist in 1977—as the orchestra's permanent conductor.

"There was no music director, no personality," he recalled. "There was nobody instilling a way to play. I knew what it would take to make it into a cohesive orchestra. I also had a lot of curiosity about repertoire." [8] Schwarz and Lockwood, until his departure from Lincoln Center in 1991, spent the ensuing seasons enlivening and enriching the festival. "The biggest problem was not finding the players," said Schwarz, "but making them into a homogenous ensemble that played together as a unit. That's a big issue with an orchestra like ours, which only operates in the summertime. We didn't have a week of rehearsal prior to the opening, nor do we now, and it takes a little time for us to learn how to play together again and remember our style." [9]

Together, Schwarz and Lockwood planned each season's programs. "My job was to make a first-class orchestra and to invigorate the repertoire," recalled Schwarz, "not to do the same pieces over and over again. That's not to say we couldn't do the *Jupiter* Symphony every year, but it is to say we could do all the other pieces too, and some early Mozart operas." [10] Each year, when they added new selections, they would identify them with an asterisk on the season's schedule.

In the summer of 1988, Schwarz and Lockwood added a full week of Haydn, which Schwarz admits to have particularly enjoyed. "In the middle of the all-Haydn week, we had a Haydn Marathon, which began at 2 in the afternoon and went until 10 or 11 at night. We covered a great variety of vocal music, chamber music and solo works. Many great artists appeared, and it was a wonderfully enjoyable event."[11]

The experimentation continued, including a hugely popular all-star Festival of Fiddlers. Schwarz also insisted on presenting Handel's *Messiah* in German; there were questions about whether it would fly in the summertime—and at the Mostly Mozart Festival, no less—but Schwarz knew his audience. It sold out. Beginning in the summer of 1991, Lincoln Center—with contributions from all of its constituents—marked the bicentennial of the composer's death by performing every Mozart composition over the course of the following year and a half. Beginning that same year, and continuing for the next nine, Mostly Mozart traveled to Tokyo.

Some prominent music critics had tired of Mostly Mozart after twenty-eight seasons, but its audiences had not, and in 1994, after rumors of its cancellation hit the newspapers, the public made its feelings known. Subsequently, the Center did pare back the festival to its original four weeks, but only to make room for the new Lincoln Center Festival, which debuted in July 1996. Mostly Mozart remained one of the Center's most reliable box-office attractions, having nurtured a faithful audience. Adding immeasurably to the visibility of Mostly Mozart, *Live from Lincoln Center* televised many of its many of its season's opening concerts.

Begun with a resident orchestra rotating with invited chamber groups, Mostly Mozart evolved, under Gerard Schwarz's leadership, into "a showcase for guest conductors and visiting ensembles."[12] Schwarz's retirement at the end of the 2001 season brought turmoil the following year: while awaiting the appointment of a new maestro and amid fears that the new conductor might want to make major changes, the Mostly Mozart Orchestra walked out in July 2002. The four-day strike forced the cancellation of two-thirds of its concerts and was settled by an agreement that called for a three-person panel to review all firing decisions and to participate in the audition process.[13]

In December 2002, Mostly Mozart welcomed the charismatic young French conductor Louis Langrée as its next musical director, and his success was immediate. "He appears to be the musical shot in the arm that the festival needs," commented one critic. "Langrée and his orchestra seem to have bonded in record time."[14] By 2004—his second season—Langrée was being credited with infusing Mostly Mozart with a new energy and spirit that audiences and critics eagerly welcomed and embraced. For its 2005 season, Langrée and Jane Moss, the Center's vice president for programming, undertook an experiment that proved highly successful: they had Avery Fisher Hall temporarily reconfigured for the Festival, extending the stage thirty feet into the hall and installing courtside seating at the sides and behind the orchestra. This was done to make the listening experience more intimate and to allow the audience, as Langreé explained, "to more fully experience the complexity, the motional nuances and the transcendence rooted in the human experience that lies at the heart of Mozart's genius."[15] Plans were under way to repeat the reconfiguration for the

2006 season, which marks the fortieth anniversary of Mostly Mozart at Lincoln Center.

Under Langrée, Mostly Mozart attendance is up, with many offerings sold out. Langrée and Moss continue to expand and develop new kinds of programming for Mostly Mozart that explores the genius of Mozart as well as the music of those who influenced him and of those whom he influenced.

INTRODUCTION.

by Jane Moss

ARTISTIC DIRECTOR, MOSTLY MOZART FESTIVAL

and Louis Langrée

RENÉE AND ROBERT BELFER MUSIC DIRECTOR

MOSTLY MOZART FESTIVAL

When Lincoln Center first launched the Mostly Mozart Festival in 1966, it was considered a radical and foolhardy idea. Common wisdom suggested that there was no summer audience in New York, and in fact an indoor summer music festival had never existed anywhere in America. Fragrant lawns, towering trees, and the night sky were considered essential for a summer musical experience. And a festival dedicated to Mozart, whose music at that time was infrequently played except for a handful of his symphonies and piano concertos, seemed an unlikely and arbitrarily narrow subject for an ongoing musical enterprise.

But from its very inception the Mostly Mozart Festival proved the skeptics wrong. Summer audiences in New York were enthusiastic and abundant. The acoustical advantages of an indoor venue, as well as its amenities, proved hugely attractive to both festival patrons and artists. Quite quickly the Mostly Mozart Festival was transformed from a radical experiment into an essential New York summer tradition and an internationally recognized success story.

And far from being too narrowly focused, the Mostly Mozart Festival succeeds precisely because of the manifold genius of Mozart himself. Uniquely posed at the juncture of several transitional musical styles, he allows us to readily traverse centuries of repertoire with clearly delineated connections and influence. Furthermore, he created extraordinary works in great quantity in all genres, providing an abundant musical treasure chest for an ongoing festival. And perhaps most important, Mozart achieved an unmatched synthesis of musical vision and the human heart. Each encounter with his music tells us more deeply about ourselves and the emotional complexity that lies at the center of the human condition.

Just as he astonished his contemporaries with his compositional gifts, Mozart continues to inspire the composers, choreographers, directors, musicians, and performers of our own time. His genius in every sense transcends time's boundaries, and he feels vitally alive among us every summer, urging us to seek and reach new pinnacles of musical achievement and innovation.

Designed for both the first-time listener and the seasoned concertgoer, *The Mostly Mozart Guide to Mozart* offers a window into Mozart's extraordinary music, revealing how—now many centuries later—it so powerfully touches and illuminates our innermost intimate landscape. Assisted by the enhanced understanding of

Mozart's achievements this guide provides, we hope the listener is able to more fully experience and embrace Mozart's music and deeply cherish, as we do, the transcendent legacy he gave to all of us.

This poster, created by Robert Motherwell, is from the Mostly Mozart Festival's Twenty-Fifth Anniversary in 1991.

PART ONE

Mozart's Biography

A HERO'S LIFE

HERE ARE ARTISTS WHOM WE ADMIRE and those whom we like, and then there is Mozart, who inspires love—for his music, of course, but also because he was so human. In every respect save one, his monumental artistic achievement, Mozart reminds us of ourselves. Often unlucky in love and constantly worried about money, he led a challenging personal life. He had to cope with family issues, especially a complicated relationship with his father, Leopold. Despite many critical and popular successes in an abbreviated career, jealousy, misunderstanding, and even scorn characterized the response of some contemporaries to Mozart's music.

Driven by Mozart's profound sense of loss, his work—as many as eight hundred compositions, depending on how you count them, in almost every musical genre—illuminates life, our joys and sorrows, our loves and our own losses. To experience one of his numerous masterpieces is to be comforted in grief, joined in celebration. Guided by his genius to reconsider what we think we know, we apprehend through Mozart's music a meaning that seems miraculously to become a mirror of ourselves.

Over the course of his life, which began in 1756 and lasted only until 1791, when he was thirty-five, Mozart managed to bequeath to the world a wealth that enriches everyone who encounters it. From what source did this wellspring come? By what pathway did this man find such greatness? Through what seeming miracle does Mozart's career and all he created bring us closer to what might be called a sense of the divine?

Not, romantic myths to the contrary, through magic. Faced with an output that by any standard of both quantity and quality is enormous, our impulse may be to ascribe such success to a kind of metaphysical alchemy, an artistic sleight of hand. This tendency, made manifest in such interpretations of Mozart as Peter Shaffer's play *Amadeus*, which was later adapted by Milos Forman into a popular movie of the same name, justly celebrates the immense technical gifts that are often characterized as God-given. Without question, Mozart was a prodigy who developed quickly into a virtuoso, as a performer as well as a composer.

To call him talented would be a giant understatement. But the speed of his development, the level it reached, and the Olympian height at which it was maintained are trivialized when explained simply as supernatural.

Throughout his career, from young childhood almost to the day he died, Mozart worked harder than anyone else around him. He never ran an arts institution, did not lead an orchestra or an opera company, and did not branch out into the kind of related ventures that typify the activities of many musical stars today. But his was a life of heroic stature precisely for the reason that against many odds, including those posed by his own demons, he earned it. And he began doing so when he was only a few years old, on the road, where rock stars and classical conductors and soloists can be found today—but hardly the usual province of a boy making his way with his father and sister through Western Europe in the eighteenth century.

What's in a Name?

Mozart's full name is a mouthful: Johannes Chrysostomus Wolfgangus Theophilus Amadeus Mozart. Today, in part because of the eponymous play and movie, Amadeus is an easily recognizable shorthand nickname for the composer. In Latin, the word means "love of god." Mozart himself sometimes used the German form of the name, Gottlieb, but his preference was a shortened form that he spelled as Amadé.

On the Road

Born in Salzburg on January 27, 1756, into a family in which he was the only surviving son, Mozart quickly became a legend in his own time. The word *prodigy* can only begin to describe the young Mozart's dazzling musical talents. Quickly mastering the pianoforte, he also taught himself how to play the violin. Before he was ten, he was writing music that challenges accomplished musicians who played it then, and continues to challenge musicians today. On hearing someone else's piece only once, he could perfectly transcribe the entire score.

Mozart's introduction to music began at home, where he was surrounded by sound. His domineering father, Leopold, was a violinist, and Mozart's older sister, Maria, called Nannerl, started piano lessons with Leopold when she was seven. Shortly afterward, and until Mozart was well into his teens, this family trio of the two siblings

Family Tree

Mozart's one surviving sibling, a sister called Nannerl, born in 1751, was more than four years older than her brother. Three other sisters were born before Mozart but all of them died in infancy, as did his two brothers. Nannerl would outlive Mozart by nearly forty years, while their parents, Maria Anna and Leopold, died nearly a decade apart from each other, in 1778 and 1787, respectively. Mozart's marriage in 1782 to Constanze Weber produced six children, only two of whom, both boys, lived past infancy.

and their dad—sometimes accompanied by their mother, Maria Anna—spent more time touring Western Europe than they did living in Salzburg. Performing before nobility and common folk, in great halls, palaces, and even a London tavern, they came into contact with such a wide cross section of people that the overall experience was to have a profound effect on the adult Mozart, both as a performer and as a composer.

Mozart's father, Leopold, performing with Mozart, who was about seven, and his older sister, Maria, called Nannerl, who was about eleven. The trio spent more time touring Western Europe than they did in Salzburg. (French engraving by De Lafosse, after Carmontelle, 1764)

During one early stretch of touring, beginning when Mozart was only six years old, the family was on the road for more than three consecutive years. Even now, such an itinerary would tax the most seasoned road warrior. But in the late eighteenth century, when roads were poor and the main form of transport was a horse-drawn carriage, the experience could be arduous, to say the least. A carriage wheel might break, an inn might have no room, a tavern poor food ... and yet the young sensation and his sister were expected not simply to perform but to dazzle.

Indeed, word of the Mozarts soon got around, and in many of the venues where they found themselves playing, the boy was tested by skeptical listeners. Already possessed of a rapidly expanding technique on the piano, Mozart also proved very early to be an adept and creative improviser. Typically, Leopold might present him with a tune, and Mozart was expected to turn it immediately into a display of variations. He was so good at this that a listener, assuming that Mozart and his father must have practiced the feat beforehand, might surprise Mozart on the spot with a new tune that he could not have heard before. Mozart never failed to pull off the stunt.

Beyond the life lessons of hard work and adaptability that Mozart learned on these tours, he came to understand the importance of pleasing an audience without compromising a principle. This lesson became a bedrock of his aesthetic and, when combined with his paternal schooling in music fundamentals and his personal sense of expression, both inspired and enabled him all his life to produce music of the highest artistic quality that also appealed to a large public. Even in the intimate confines of a small village church where he

Mozart the prodigy, shown here performing in Vienna, was often tested by skeptical listeners. Whether he knew a tune or was surprised with one that he had never heard before, the young Mozart could immediately turn it into a set of variations. (Engraving by Gustave Boulanger)

improvised for a tiny gathering of people, Mozart was a crowd-pleaser.

Because musicians of his era depended so heavily on the patronage of the wealthy, many of Mozart's acquaintances, if not friends, were members of the nobility. But he never lost the common touch, remaining comfortable in the company of other musicians and their families. He was especially at home with people of the theater—costume makers, stagehands, and the like—because they worked as well in opera, the musical genre in which Mozart enjoyed some of his greatest triumphs. Later in his life, when he became a Mason, he made friends easily among the members of his Masonic lodge.

Lights, Camera, Action

Entertaining, and with a sound track of the composer's greatest hits, the film *Amadeus,* based on the play
of the same name, presents a misleading interpretation
of Mozart's life and personality. Starring Tom Hulce as
Mozart and F. Murray Abraham as his rival, Antonio
Salieri, the film depicts a buffoonlike Mozart whose
death was the result of poisoning by Salieri—a rumor
of long historical standing, that is generally discredited
by modern scholars. Interestingly, the story was first
dramatized by the Russian poet Alexander Pushkin,
and his play was later made into an opera by his fellow
countryman Nikolai Rimsky-Korsakov. Among the other
inaccuracies of the film is the mistaken presentation of
Salieri completing Mozart's last work, the unfinished
requiem that Mozart was writing on his deathbed.

Home in Salzburg

Not until 1773, when Mozart was seventeen—having
already lived, it would turn out, nearly half of his short
life—did he settle down for a protracted period in the
provincial city of Salzburg, a place he despised. By then,
his travels had taken him three times to Italy, with many
other trips to places as diverse as Prague, the Hague,
Paris, London, and Vienna, where he would move per-
manently in 1781.

Although Salzburg has long been part of Austria, in
Mozart's day it was a political entity unto itself, gov-
erned by a nobility tied to the church. In 1772, Count

The Mozart House in Salzburg where Mozart was born. He despised the provincial city, and after he left to settle in Vienna, he returned to visit only once—to introduce his wife, Constanze, to his family. (Unsigned drawing)

Hieronymus von Colloredo had become Salzburg's archbishop, and his autocratic patronage of Mozart did less to sustain the young composer than to strengthen his desire to depart.

Leopold Mozart held the title of court composer, conferred on him by Colloredo's predecessor, Sigismund von Schrattenbach, and by this time Mozart himself had been appointed *Konzertmeister*, though initially without pay. Over the years during their travels, father and son had angled for various other positions, both honorific and paid, because this was a chief form of support for most musicians. It was a hard way to make a living, with the usual intrigues and jealousies compounded in Mozart's

Where Is Mozart?

Mozart, according to the late lexicographer and writer Nicolas Slonimsky, is the only classical composer after whom a town has been named. Located in the Canadian province of Saskatchewan, the town of Mozart has a population of fewer than fifty people. All of its street names honor other composers.

case by Colloredo's evident antipathy. The man had a cold heart and tin ears.

Nevertheless, with the exception of regular but much less frequent forays elsewhere, Mozart during this period put up with the small-mindedness of his hometown, while performing often and writing music of ever higher quality at an ever increasing pace. But as soon as he could, and despite his father's attempts to keep him from doing so, he would leave Salzburg for good.

Perhaps the most striking aspect of Mozart's extended Salzburg residence is how outwardly commonplace it appears to have been. Mozart was never involved in a scandal. As far as we know, he never broke the law. Though he was once sued late in his life for the repayment of a loan, he never initiated a legal claim on someone else. If there had been cable television news or tabloids when he was alive, he would have made very poor copy. In a pattern that would persist even after he moved to Vienna, Mozart's main activity was making music. To relax, he might smoke his pipe or enjoy a glass of wine, and he became something of a billiards expert, eventually owning his own billiards table. Were it not for his music, however, he might have been noticed only for the fine clothes he favored.

Vienna and the World

In his early twenties, Mozart continued to travel, on one occasion in 1778 to France with his mother, where she died at the age of fifty-eight. Mozart did not at first report

Romance

Mozart enjoyed the company of women, although there is little evidence in his correspondence or that of his contemporaries of numerous liaisons. In part, this may have been the result of his father's fear that love affairs would sidetrack his son's musical progress. But it seems just as possible that Mozart simply found few women with whom he was capable of sustaining a long-term relationship. In fact, the only woman who had a lasting romance with Mozart was his wife, Constanze Weber, whom he married in 1782 (and with whose older sister Aloysia Mozart had earlier been in love). That marriage, opposed by Leopold, would be tested by the couple's financial problems and the poor health of Constanze. There is a conspicuous lack of documentation about their time together during Mozart's last years, but the letters Mozart wrote to Constanze near the end of his life are passionate.

Constanze Weber, whom Mozart married in 1782. The marriage, which his father, Leopold, opposed, would be tested by the couple's financial problems and Constanze's poor health. (Lithograph of an oil painting by Joseph Lange, 1798)

this sad family loss to his father, Leopold. Eventually, however, the loyal son returned again to Salzburg, where the two men continued in the employ of Archbishop Colloredo. Mozart increasingly viewed his own duties as servitude, chafing under the archbishop's dictums, which often struck Mozart as whims. By the time he was twenty-five, he was determined to find a way out.

The pathway that presented itself was his music, which by this time had reached a level far beyond anything even Leopold could have imagined. Now a pianist of gathering renown, Mozart was rapidly consolidating a reputation as a composer of extraordinary music. Just how this happened is one of the great riddles of artistic creation; Mozart himself left very few hints, as if he himself could not explain a brilliance that was already becoming a preeminence.

Theories abound, but surely one, though incomplete, is the well-founded fact of his remarkable ability to concentrate. In addition, Mozart worked at an astonishingly fast speed; rarely was he stumped, and even then only by his singular standard would a Mozartean pause be construed as delay. Supremely self-confident, Mozart was not one to wallow in existential doubt; he knew what he could do, and he went about it quickly and with conviction.

And with amazing results. Before an intemperate exchange with the archbishop forced his dismissal from his position, Mozart had already composed most of his symphonies, several operas, numerous sacred works, many concertos for both piano and violin, and a miscellany of other pieces that ranged from clever canons to beautiful serenades. He was also, by his late teens, composing music that to our ears sounds indisputably like . . . Mozart: he had, in other words, found his musical voice at a very young age.

One of the ancillary wonders of Mozart's move to Vienna reflects a cultural phenomenon that, posed as a sociological question, may be larger even than the wonder of Mozart. And that question, simply put, is how on a scale of contemporary population and historical background a city of such relatively small size as Vienna

MUSINGS ON

Victor Borge with a revisionist account of how Mozart met Constanze

The one thing Mozart needed more than a good libretto was a good wife. "The voice of nature speaks as loud in me as in others," he wrote his father, "louder, perhaps, than in many a big strong lout of a fellow." Wolfgang's problem, by his own admission, was that he was too much of a gentleman to seduce an innocent girl, and too much of a coward to risk catching something from a non-innocent girl, and all his father could ever say was Practice, Practice, Practice. Just before his twenty-second birthday, Wolfgang finally met the girl of his dreams. Her name was Aloysia Weber, and she was sixteen and sang beautifully and even played the harpsichord a little, and it was love at first sonata. As usual, Papa Mozart was aghast at anything that might take Wolfgang's mind off his music, and he ordered his son to go off on another concert tour immediately. Rumors of the romance were still floating around when Wolfgang returned, nearly a year later, but then Aloysia became the mistress of the Elector of Salzburg, and afterwards she married an actor named Lange. That stopped the rumors. Still, Mozart had his heart set on marrying a Weber, and since there were three sisters left in the family, he moved in with all of them so he shouldn't make any mistakes this time. Eventually he picked Constanze, who was far from pretty and anything but bright and shabbily dressed most of the time. "But she understands housekeeping," Mozart explained when he wrote home asking his father's permission for the wedding.

From *My Favorite Intermissions* (with Robert Sherman, 1971)

either produced or, in Mozart's case, for a time supported an art that now encircles the globe. What made this possible?

Possible answers are plentiful, but first a qualifier, one that raises the same question but with a different locale. During the decade (1781–1791) when Mozart lived and, for the most part, prospered artistically in Vienna, his greatest public following was actually in Prague. It was to Prague that Mozart traveled to hear performances of his *Marriage of Figaro* in early 1787, on a visit that produced a symphony (no. 38, K. 504) that today bears the city's name and triggered a commission for *Don Giovanni*. And it was in Prague, not in Vienna, that the greatest public outpouring of grief occurred after Mozart's death.

You've Got Mail

Mozart grew up in a family of letter writers and the correspondence between Mozart and his father provides rich documentation for much of Mozart's life and career. Mozart's first letter that has been saved, a short note to a girlfriend, was written when he was thirteen, and the last was to his wife, written less than two months before he died.

Published in 1938 (and updated in 1985), the first English translation of the letters, by Emily Anderson, remains for many the definitive text, containing more than six hundred of Mozart's letters. There have been other translations and selections, including a wonderful merging of Mozart's biography and a lively, new translation of his letters by Robert Spaethling, published in 2000. Overall, the letters tell us little about the mystery of Mozart's artistic mastery and creativity. But they engagingly convey the immense range of Mozart's work, his travels, and his professional and personal relationships, including a somewhat notorious flirtation with a younger cousin, Maria Anna Thekla Mozart, or Bäsle. They also ground our sense of Mozart and his family, particularly his father, making their daily struggles with, and victories over, the exigencies of hearth and home, room and board, friend and foe, seem real to us.

Mozart's younger cousin Maria Anna Thekla Mozart, with whom he carried on a rather notorious flirtation. (Unsigned pencil drawing, 1777/1778)

"I have so much to do already," Mozart wrote from Paris in 1778 to his father (in Anderson's translation), "that I wonder what it will be like in winter!" And he went on, in a long letter characteristic of the family correspondence, to discuss his work, what he was being paid, and some of the personalities he had just encountered, before closing with this typical flourish: "Adieu. I kiss your hands 100,000 times and embrace my sister with all my heart . . . I remain your most obedient son."

Intriguingly, there are periods of Mozart's life—particularly, the final years—wherein relatively few of his letters have been preserved. Although any number of ideas might be advanced to explain this, it is likely that after his father's death in 1787, Mozart had less incentive to report on his activities, because his father had been his primary correspondent. Even so, an air of mystery springs from the absence of letters during such crucial moments of his career as the summer of 1788, when in the space of just three months Mozart wrote his last three symphonies—a summer during which only a single letter to his sister and a few to a friend asking for money are extant.

But it was in Vienna that Mozart (and Constanze) lived, often moving within the city center and sometimes to one of the suburbs. Vienna had first been settled more than a thousand years before Mozart's birth in Salzburg and by the late eighteenth century was a city-state of more than two hundred thousand people. Its dominant religion was Catholicism, in no small part

Vienna at the end of the eighteenth century. (Unsigned engraving)

a vestige of an earlier time when Vienna was the capital of the Holy Roman Empire. Long before Mozart arrived on the scene to take up permanent residence, many of the city's most beautiful buildings had been erected, including the Burgtheater, where Mozart would present the first performances of three of his operas.

Court life, around which so much of the city's musical heritage was centered, was provincial and political, and a huge portion of Mozart's energy seems to have been devoted to dealing with intrigue and reputation. To a degree that is difficult to calibrate exactly, a good deal of Mozart's ongoing financial distress can be attributed to the necessity, as he saw it, of keeping up appearances. Thus, the brilliant composer and celebrated performer always felt that he had to dress the part; Mozart spent large sums on clothing, and he even owned his own carriage.

His music was increasingly popular with the general population, particularly because of the success of his operas. Numerous stories recount instances of common folk singing their favorite arias from Mozart's works. Nevertheless, the total number of people who could have known the music firsthand had to have been rather small, even after adding in those from other cities that he continued to visit as an adult. Yet somehow the word—or, rather, the song—spread. Unlike Bach, much of whose music went unplayed for long periods after his death, Mozart has never gone out of fashion, and the city where he lived from the age of twenty-five until his death at thirty-five vies with the city of his birth in claiming him as its own. The only remaining building in Vienna where Mozart lived is now a museum, and the Vienna Tourist Board touts a walking tour of places that Mozart would have frequented or known.

Except for a visit after his marriage to introduce Constanze to his father and sister, Mozart never again returned to Salzburg. During the decade when Mozart lived in Vienna, he composed masterpiece after masterpiece, including his four greatest operas, his finest symphonies, numerous chamber and incidental works, transformational piano concertos, and the Requiem, on which he was working before his death, probably from rheumatic fever. That death, on December 5, 1791, was followed by burial in a common grave, which was the custom then in Vienna and not, contrary to fanciful accounts, a kind of pauper's funeral. Nor was the occasion ignored by the greater populace. Ten days after Mozart's death, Nicolai Church

"The life of Mozart is the triumph of genius over precociousness."

—Peter Gay, biographer of Mozart

in Prague—the city of several of Mozart's most noteworthy triumphs—was filled to overflowing with men and women mourning the end of Mozart's life and celebrating the miracle of his musical immortality.

Chronology

January 27, 1756	Mozart born in Salzburg
January 1762	First trip (to Munich), with sister, Nannerl, and father, Leopold
September 1762	First visit to Vienna; first recorded compositions
June 1763	Beginning of Mozart family's three-year European tour
1768	First full-length opera, *La finta semplice* (The Pretended Simpleton), K. 51
1771	Piano Concerto in E-flat, K. 271
Late 1772–early 1773	Third Italian tour
1778	Mozart's mother, Maria Anna, dies while with him in Paris
1781	Two operas: *Idomeneo*, K. 366; *Die Entführung aus dem Serail* (The Abduction from the Seraglio), K. 384; Mozart moves permanently to Vienna

1782	Marriage to Constanze Weber
1786	*Le nozze di Figaro* (The Marriage of Figaro), K. 492
1787	Leopold Mozart dies; *Don Giovanni*, K. 527
1788	Last three symphonies: nos. 39, 40, and 41 (K. 543, K. 550, and K. 551)
1790	*Così fan tutte* (Women Are Like That), K. 588
1791	*Die Zauberflöte* (The Magic Flute), K. 620; Requiem (unfinished), K. 626; dies December 5

Mozart's Works

LET THERE BE MUSIC

I F YOU WERE THE DIRECTOR OF
a major symphony orchestra, you could
program works only by Mozart for an entire year
and barely exhaust the supply. If you were to
attempt to do the same with Gustav Mahler's
works, you'd run out of material in about three
months; with Frédéric Chopin, you'd quickly
need to send the orchestra home and simply
present piano recitals; were your choice Franz
Schubert, you'd soon be focused on solo singers.
Once you got past his nine symphonies and

a few choral works, even Ludwig van Beethoven would be a stretch, as would Johannes Brahms, whose symphonic output ended with his fourth. Joseph Haydn could handle the challenge, although your audiences might begin to become restless after the first few dozen symphonies. Probably only Johann Sebastian Bach wrote an amount of music comparable to Mozart's of such excellence and variety though it would be a reach to call the great man entertaining.

From his late teens until nearly the end of his life, Mozart wrote some of the finest, most beautiful symphonies of any composer in history; three of his operas are indisputably among the greatest ever created; most of his twenty-six piano concertos are models of elegant form and emotional impact. With his stupendous

MUSINGS ON

Rob Kapilow on Mozart's spirit of complexity

In a quotation that always comes to mind when I think of Mozart, the brilliant Czech writer Milan Kundera said, "The novel's spirit is the spirit of complexity. Every novel says to the reader: things are not as simple as you think." And the same can be said of Mozart's music. No matter how simple it seems, it is never as simple as you think. Mozart's music is never as symmetrical, regular, or conventional as it appears to be; it takes close listening to notice the subtle irregularities and hidden asymmetries that make his music so great. Mozart's music is like a sublimely balanced hologram—it is both simple and complicated at the same

range, Mozart also composed concertos for violin, flute, clarinet, and horn, as well as numerous solo works for piano, chamber music, dance music, serenades, songs, canons, masses, and the famed final work, the Requiem Mass in D Minor. All of this music is distinguished by its intelligence and logic, by a directness that seems to belie its technical complexity and mastery, and by a kind of seamless integration of parts in which the relationship of different instruments or of ensemble and soloist is always of a piece. Mozart never wrote mere accompaniment; *décor* was not in his musical vocabulary.

Nor is his music ever sentimental. He not only eschewed cheap effects but, based on the evidence, was also incapable of them. In composition after composition,

---

time. When the surface looks straightforward, tuneful, and regular, the phrase structure is almost always subtly irregular underneath. However, when the surface seems jarring and disorienting, there is almost always regularity underneath. Mozart's universe is both surprising and understandable at the same time. As our culture tends more and more to deal with complex issues in black-and-white, sound-bite fashion, we have Mozart to remind us that things are never as "simple as you think."

Rob Kapilow is a conductor and a composer, and the author of *All You Have to Do Is Listen*

---

we hear a man who gets immediately to the heart of whatever it is he wishes to say, yet never takes a shortcut to get there. Retrospectively, we can see what appears to be the inevitability of his accomplishment, but when we listen it is as if the music is always on the cusp of making a new discovery, fresh as the promise of another dawn.

Born of a brave, constantly exposed vulnerability, everything in the mature Mozart is there for a reason. This most sociable of composers, who for most of his career had to depend on the kindness of others for financial support, had many friends but virtually no peers. Haydn was a fan, but he was older and by the end of Mozart's life was living in London. Beethoven was still a boy when Mozart moved from Salzburg to Vienna, and they would meet just once, when Mozart had only four years left to live. Whether by accident or, more probably, as a consequence of his loneliness, Mozart's music conveys a strong sense of longing. That aesthetic, if one may characterize it in this way, is at once the record of a solitary soul and the revelation of one person's temporary conquest of our mutual mortality.

To grapple in Mozart's music with the how of the why and what—with the means, in other words, that enabled him to achieve his ends—is to reflect, in a sense, on the very nature not simply of creativity but of creation itself. Unlike most artists, once Mozart reached his maturity—a slightly ludicrous term, since his life ended when he was still a relatively young man—he did not so much develop or shift from one period to another as manifest ever greater depths of profundity and grandeur. He was, to put it differently, already fully formed as an artist at a time in life when others are still learning their craft, defining their ambition, weathering the usual vicissitudes of self-doubt and angst.

Köchel Numbers

Though Mozart kept a dated ledger of his work, he was far too busy and prolific to keep track of all the music he wrote. Nor was he psychologically predisposed to slog through the enormous task of tabulating his output. Especially toward the end of his life, he preferred spending a free evening with a lovely soprano to sorting a box of musical manuscripts. Thus, it fell to a nineteenth-century Austrian scientist, Ludwig von Köchel, to catalog in chronological order Mozart's oeuvre, giving each piece what came to be called a Köchel, or K., number. The catalog has been revised frequently since it first appeared in 1862. In the current, eighth edition several compositions have been given a new number, so that they are sometimes identified with two different numbers, one following the other. The original numeration ends with K. 626, the Requiem in D Minor, but many of the K. numbers are for works consisting of several separate pieces; were they all counted as distinct compositions, the total would exceed eight hundred.

Symphonies and Orchestral Works

It was early in the summer of 1788, and Mozart, thirty-two, felt that he had nothing to lose. He was broke; the iffy health of his wife, Constanze, required frequent cures and rest at her favorite spa; and their infant daughter, Theresia, born the previous December, was not well. Musically, Mozart's career seemed in something of a stasis. His great opera *Don Giovanni*, which had premiered in Prague the previous year to prolonged acclaim, had just begun a sporadic run in Vienna with a few performances in May. The emperor, distracted by the prospect of war with Turkey, had pronounced the music difficult, while the public, though positive in its response, reserved its highest praise for the work of several other composers who are today forgotten. What to do?

Whether on his own initiative or through the intervention of a patron—we can't be certain because the historical record for most of this important year is missing—Mozart turned to the musical form he knew best: the symphony. There would be some subscription performances later in the summer, or such was the apparent idea; again, evidence that these concerts ever took place is scant. But the fact that Mozart got to work is undeniable. Even for him, what he ended up producing was beyond exceptional.

Since childhood, Mozart had been writing symphonies, although the first few were of interest chiefly because they had been composed by someone so young. Scholars have not come to full agreement over how much input Mozart's father, Leopold, had into those early efforts, which also included some of his initial works for piano and a number of liturgical compositions, but sometime around his seventeenth birthday, Mozart suddenly began producing music that wasn't just good but also sounded . . . new. He composed a ravishingly beautiful church piece, *Exsultate, jubilate*, K. 165, for soprano, orchestra, and organ, as well as a lovely work for two violins and orchestra, K. 190, which he called Concertone. His symphonic output followed suit, with an architectural expansion from three to four movements, wider variety in the orchestration, an increasing complexity in the counterpoint, and a significantly enlarged emotional resonance.

Fifteen years later, Mozart's mastery of the form was complete, and, writing music in a style that is always recognizable as his, Mozart revolutionized the symphony in just the short space of one summer. He wrote three—nos. 39, 40, and 41—between June and August 1788, and

> The very perfection of Mozart's last three symphonies . . . is miraculous, and the more so given how quickly they were composed. No less impressive is their diversity, and the clarity with which, in three quite different directions, they define the possibilities of Mozart's art."
>
> —Michael Steinberg, author of *The Symphony*, was the program annotator for several orchestras.

each one is a masterwork. To listen to these symphonies, singly or, as is often the case in concert, with all three on the same program, is to be struck immediately and simultaneously by their melodic lyricism, their rhythmic dynamism, their textured orchestration, and their harmonious, transparent sound. They create a world that invites—no, commands—entry. Anyone can come in.

The symphonic world Mozart entered as a boy was a codified maze of highly formalized structure and limited emotional range. The composer, often a hired gun to

What Did Mozart Hear?

One anomaly of Mozart's final three symphonies is that so far as musicologists have been able to ascertain, they were not written on demand. Circumstantial evidence suggests that Mozart expected to be presenting them as part of a subscription series, but if the concerts ever took place there is no proof. One modern scholar has analyzed the different papers on which Mozart wrote the music, in order to determine whether their composition might have taken place over a longer period of time than is usually accepted. Most Mozart scholars still conclude that just as Beethoven never heard his ninth, because he was deaf, Mozart never heard his forty-first, the *Jupiter*, and probably not the thirty-ninth, either. His rival, Antonio Salieri, did conduct two performances of the popular fortieth in Vienna during April 1791, and it is quite possible that Mozart was in attendance.

entertain the nobility, was expected to navigate a basically predetermined pathway, an end, with a given set of means. More often than not, the result was music that simply passed the time of the listener, with extra credit given for logical coherence, clever manipulation, and occasional brashness. The more intelligent the composer, the greater likelihood that he—and every composer in those days was a he—would succeed in coming up with something that was just a little bit different from the efforts of others or even from his own previous work. But too much originality was frowned on; in fact, the very modern idea that creativity enhances one's stature or reputation was foreign. No artistes, in other words. The composer in Mozart's youth was basically a craftsman.

There were, of course, exceptions, notably Haydn when Mozart arrived on the scene. And certainly in performance on musical instruments, talent was acknowledged, if not prized. The music itself, however, might surprise a little but should not shock, and its glory should reflect on its patron, not its maker, or should be directed toward praise for the Almighty.

Through extensive tutelage from his domineering father, Leopold, from the other music he heard and the musicians he met through their touring, and simply by virtue of his own common sense, the young Mozart understood this. But had that been the extent of his understanding, it is certain that music as we know it would be very different. Though such grand generalizations can mislead, the entire century-long Romantic period that Beethoven ushered in is partly traceable in its origins to the impact of Mozart. Impossible to imagine a Brahms who did not know the *Jupiter* Symphony, a Berlioz who was not inspired by the example of Mozart's

How Mozart Composed

One of the many mysteries about Mozart's prodigious output is the sheer size of it, given the shortness of his life and the amount of time that most composers typically need to complete a piece. According to the twentieth-century Mozart scholar Alfred Einstein, whose 1945 book about the composer was for many years the definitive biographical text available in English, the methods Mozart used were unusual, to say the least. In contrast to the typical composer who works everything out, measure by measure, often as he or she sits at the piano, Mozart seems to have viewed the act of composing as more of a mental exercise, as if the actual writing out of a new piece were more a matter of taking dictation.

"The filo, the thread that Mozart follows," Einstein wrote, "is so dependent upon the right beginning; the beginning must be the very best." And so, Einstein continued, "Mozart has this filo in his head before he starts to write: all witnesses of Mozart at work agree that he put a composition down on paper as one writes a letter, without allowing any disturbance or interruption to annoy him—the writing down, the fixing, was nothing more than that—the fixing of the completed work a mechanical act. Mozart's procedure during this process is easily followed, thanks to his frequent changes to fresh-cut quills and the varying colors of the ink, which evidently thickened quickly and had to be thinned out or freshened very often. Mozart never writes subparts or sections of a movement, complete in all voices,

Mozart as a young composer. He began to compose as a child, but how he managed to create such a prodigious output, given his short life and the time most composers need to complete a piece, remains a mystery. (Painting by Joseph-Siffred Duplessis)

but always a whole. Sketch and final form blend into one act of writing; he does not make rough drafts. In an opera score, for instance—not merely in an aria or a short ensemble, a quartet or sextet, but even in an extended ensemble—he writes out the first violin, the voices and the bass, beginning to end; only then does he fill in subordinate parts, and one can trace stroke by stroke how even during such half mechanical labor the joy of inventing details, of inspiration, never forsakes him. (Of course, where the orchestral part contains solo passages for the wind instruments, these are included in the first writing.) In a work of chamber music, or a symphony, he fixes first the principal voices, the melodic threads, from beginning to end, leaping as it were from line to line, and inserting the subordinate voices only when he goes over or overhauls the movement in a second stage of the procedure."

daring, a Bruckner who was not moved by Mozart's example, a Mahler whose ambition was not nourished by the passion of his composing forebear.

Virtually every musician we listen to today owes some kind of debt to Mozart, karmic or otherwise. And while it may be somewhat superficial to separate the influence of Mozart's oeuvre into categories, because they all overlap in both their chronology and their development, it is indisputable that his symphonic output, particularly in its final phase, changed the course of music history.

Hints of later developments abound here and there in Mozart's earliest symphonic work, and one of the pleasures of listening to those pieces is detecting evidence of what's to come. Nowhere is this more apparent than in the second movement of his Symphony no. 27 in G Major, K. 183, one of six he produced in 1773, when he was just seventeen years old. Based on the kind of folk melody Mozart might have heard while traveling through the Austrian countryside, the graceful, lilting Andantino grazioso lasts no more than five minutes. And yet in that brief time the listener feels transported, always with a sense that the moment will be gone.

ALTHOUGH SOME CONDUCTORS HAVE ignored Mozart's symphonies, recordings, even of the early symphonies alone, are too numerous to list completely. A splendid recounting of Symphony no. 27—and everything symphonic that came before and after it—is available in a set by the Prague Chamber Orchestra, conducted by Sir Charles Mackerras, who has also compiled an extensive Mozart oeuvre with the Scottish Chamber Orchestra. The late Viennese conductor Josef Krips capped his career with recordings for Philips, now hard to find, of what he classified as Mozart's mature symphonies, but they include several of the works Mozart composed while still in his teens. Also notable are the comprehensive surveys by Jeffrey Tate with the English Chamber Orchestra on EMI and Trevor Pinnock with the English Concert on Deutsche Grammophon.

Although it is customarily documented that Mozart composed forty-one symphonies, a true tally depends in part on how and what one counts. In addition to questions about whether Papa Mozart might have helped his son on some of his first symphonic efforts, there are several existing symphonic fragments, documents referring to symphonies Mozart either never got around to writing or those whose scores he had misplaced, and an additional few symphonies that were at first mistakenly thought to be Mozart's.

After the youthful exercises and adolescent advances, Mozart greatly slowed the pace of his symphonic writing. But the quality of what he wrote zoomed ever higher, from around the composition of his *Paris* Symphony, no. 31, K. 297. The piece was written and first performed during the summer of 1778 in Paris, where Mozart was

Mozart's father, Leopold. Some believe that he helped Mozart with some of his first symphonies. (Unsigned drawing)

visiting with his mother—a fateful visit, because she became ill and died before they set forth for home.

Three more symphonies followed in the next two years before, in 1782, at the age of twenty-six, Mozart composed his *Haffner* Symphony, no. 35, K. 385, the first of six final symphonies that would define him forever as a supreme master of the form.

Pretend, if you will, that Mozart was a kind of time traveler visiting us here, as the beauty of these symphonies surges softly into melody, harmony, a sense of meaning, an anchor in this crazy world, an affirmation right on the edge between honest fright and complete rapture. To accept the music's invitation as an invocation is to trust it, trust its maker, the spine-tingling opening scales of the thirty-ninth or the tension of the forty-first's Andante growing suddenly as we begin to imagine homes, hospitals, roads, streets, avenues—people, their goodness as well as their demons, made manifest by the music. This music remains true and relevant, as if Mozart somehow anticipated how it would feel to be alive in the new millennium, a world that the composer of this music could never have imagined even in a dream. And yet, listening to this music in, say, the vast open space of an auditorium without walls, where the wind in the tall pines beyond the lawn on either side provides an accompaniment, or in a gleaming new downtown hall, a school auditorium, your car, or the living room in your home, is to be taken to the very edge of the abyss and back again.

The *Haffner* Symphony that we know today is not actually the one that Mozart first conducted in 1782 on the occasion of a celebration in the family of the onetime mayor of Salzburg, Sigmund Haffner. Mozart had earlier written what became known as the "Haffner Serenade"

The Once and Future Masters

Born in Bonn, Germany, less than a generation after Mozart, Beethoven was seventeen in 1787 when a friend arranged for him to travel to Vienna and meet the man on whose symphonic achievement he would soon begin to build. Accounts of their single meeting are sketchy, but according to Mozart's most important nineteenth-century biographer, Otto Jahn, Beethoven was brought to Mozart's home, where he was asked to improvise on the piano for the thirty-one-year-old master. Mozart, who was initially skeptical, according to Jahn, supposedly remarked afterward that Beethoven would one day "give the world something to talk about."

Throughout most of his adult life Mozart accepted pupils, in both piano and composition. But if he was inclined to take on Beethoven after that audition, the opportunity did not arise. Learning only two weeks after his arrival in Vienna that his mother's already precarious health had taken a turn for the worse, Beethoven was summoned home by his father. Not until five years later, in 1792, did Beethoven return to the great cultural center of continental Europe. By then, alas, it was too late for a second meeting between the once and future masters; Mozart was dead.

when the mayor's sister was married, and his initial intention in 1782 was simply to write another serenade, which he did. Mozart subsequently revised this piece a few months later into the symphony as we know it.

Like the *Haffner* that preceded it and the *Prague* that followed, the *Linz* Symphony, no. 36, K. 425, also grew out of an event, a pattern that was typical of Mozart during most of his career. Whatever the inspiration that drove him to take his music to places where no other composer had ever been, the impetus to create was almost always a commission or a concert. Frenetically busy from early childhood on, Mozart really had no time for idle creativity. Had there been such a place during his lifetime, he would not have been a resident at a colony for artists. Mozart wrote music that was at once a salvation, a redemption, a revelation, and not incidentally an

Mozart's "Missing" Thirty-seventh

For many years, an unnamed symphony in G major, supposedly composed in 1783, was ascribed to Mozart and listed as K. 444 in the original Köchel catalog. By the early twentieth century, it was clear to scholars that except for the symphony's introductory Adagio, the piece was the work of Joseph Haydn's brother Michael, an important presence in the musical life of Salzburg. Joseph Haydn, to whom Mozart would dedicate his most famous string quartets, was both friend and fan of his younger fellow composer. Effusive with a father's pride, Leopold Mozart reported that Joseph Haydn called Wolfgang the greatest composer he knew or had ever heard of.

inspiration to the creativity of others, but for the man himself music was first and foremost a job.

In the case of his *Linz* Symphony, there was the little matter of a concert for which Mozart had not realized that musicians had already been engaged. Mozart and his new bride, Constanze, had just arrived at Linz in late October 1783. Their host, a count with a tongue twister of a name, Johann Thun-Hohenstein, informed Mozart that he was expected to present a symphony on November 4. With no alternative, because he had not brought the scores for any of his symphonies with him, Mozart wrote what became the *Linz* Symphony in four days. Even for him, this was a remarkable feat; had the music he produced been routine, simply to get so many notes on paper in such a short time would still have been stupendous. But the piece turned out to be one of his best, by turns buoyant and lyrical, and with an inventiveness and an underlying tension. It trumped the *Haffner*, while foreshadowing the great *Prague*, which came three years later, in 1786.

The *Prague* Symphony, no. 38, K. 504, emerged from a conducting engagement that Mozart had in the beautiful city of that name in January 1787. Mozart's opera *The Marriage of Figaro* was in the middle of a highly popular run in Prague, and Mozart had been invited to conduct several of the performances. A concert in which he would perform on the piano was also scheduled, and there is some thought that Mozart at one point intended to present an adaptation of his *Paris* Symphony at this event. Instead, in December, before traveling to Prague with his wife and her sister,

here is no traveling music in Mozart. Every note is important."

—Wynton Marsalis

48

he composed an entire new work. Like many of his earliest symphonies, the *Prague* is missing a minuet and thus has only three movements. But this similarity of structure is perhaps its only likeness to its precursors. The piece plumbs emotional depths hitherto explored by Mozart only, for the most part, in opera and piano and therefore more than hints at the symphonic immensity to follow in 1788.

The mysterious summer of 1788 looms as an epoch unto itself in Mozart's career. Very little about this time in his mostly well-documented career is known; no Mozart letters from this period survive, except for one to his sister, Nannerl, and repeated entreaties for money to Michael Puchberg, a Masonic friend. Mozart was thirty-two then, with only three years of his short but hugely productive life left; his father had died the year before, and he was broke, which among other things obliged him to move from one Vienna suburb to another.

If he wanted to change his life, there were worse ways than by composing the extraordinary, repeated, descending scales that open the first movement of his Symphony no. 39, K. 543. Mozart completed the piece on June 26, 1788, three days before his six-month-old daughter, Theresia, died. *Three days.* Who could possibly grasp how Mozart truly felt and how he put those feelings in his music? It is the central question, the ultimate inscrutability, of his art.

In the department of musical miracles, the thirty-ninth symphony and the two that soon followed, no. 40 in July and no. 41 in August, stand together as one of the grand human achievements in all the arts. If he had done nothing else, we would still cite them now, so many years later. In these exceptional works, Mozart not only entertains but also helps us make our own way through the perils and pleasures of living. To experience them is to understand immediately why Mozart and his music are modern, intimate with every aspect of human life. The development and resolution of the conflicting forces that drive their ambition, the balance of melodic function and harmonic form that brings forth beauty: all trace back, Mozart seems to be saying in these last symphonies, to the acceptance of our mortality. But do we create in part because we know we will die?

Mozart never answers such questions directly but instead leaves clues in such moments as his employment of a Baroque hemiola in the slow movement of his *Jupiter* Symphony. A rhythmic device often used by Bach, a hemiola takes two measures written in the meter of 3/4 (three beats to a measure, with a quarter note having the value of a single beat) and makes them sound as one measure in 3/2 (again, three beats to a measure, but with a half note getting a full beat). Anyone listening immediately recognizes that something unusual is going on, with accents on each half note. The heartbeat of this seemingly mixed meter creates tension, not merely musical tension but human tension. And then the tension is released, enabling Mozart to make this moment in his music a supreme example of letting go, the very thing, by this time in his life, that he had to do with the death of another child.

Of course, the musical vocabulary of these symphonies also defines and turns on numerous other relationships among such matters as the tonic (the "home" key of each piece), the integration of other keys within the overall structure of each symphony, and the seamless alteration and variation of tempi. All of this relates to and resonates within the constant search through the music for meaning and permanence, demarcating a pathway of vicissitudes large and small, both the big crises and day-to-day struggles. Mozart in these magnificent symphonies brings each of us full square to face a sometimes terrifying truth: the answer to the question "Who am I?" After an immersion in these works, we sense a man as vital as this life-giving, gorgeous music, a man for whom the oneness of sadness and joy mirrors the closeness of art and experience.

To put the achievement of Mozart's mature symphonic output in further perspective, consider simply the scale of his achievement in comparison to that of others. Although Mozart's late symphonies are shorter

Sound Effects

Musicians for many years have tried to imitate the way the symphonic music of the mature Mozart sounds. As far as one can tell, no Mozartean version of P. D. Q. Bach has yet emerged. P. D. Q. Bach is the fictitious name of a talented musical mimic, Peter Schickele, whose imitations of Johann Sebastian Bach owe their hilarity in part to Schickele's uncanny ability to replicate Bach's harmonic structures. In Mozart's case, however, there is the further challenge of figuring out how he employed or combined the instruments he had at hand, strings and winds, with the additional accompaniment of tympani and sometimes a valveless trumpet or two.

Although Mozart was a string player by training and a pianist by profession, he had an uncanny sense of how different complements of woodwinds affected the overall sound of his music. Part of this knowledge must have grown out of the great works he composed for winds alone. But Mozart was also an originator in the ways he wrote for winds within his orchestras, especially in how he created "sound effects" through the manipulation of string-wind sonorities. Much of his music's grace grows out of this ability and its transparency—the clarity of line within the harmony that makes any moment of a Mozart symphony indisputably his and impossibly anyone else's.

than, say, most of those by Beethoven or Brahms—and much shorter than those of Bruckner or Mahler—he wrote them practically in his spare time. Yes, these other composers were busy and, depending on how you calculate, prolific. But, to take Mahler as the most extreme example, apart from some superb songs and one string quartet, in a life that lasted fifty years, his entire musical output consisted of nine finished symphonies, plus a symphonic song cycle (*Das Lied von der Erde* [The Song of the Earth]) that might as well have been called a symphony and an unfinished tenth symphony.

These days, were a composer to apply for a grant or receive a commission for a symphony, she or he might work on it for the better part of a year. Yet, as far as we know, Mozart wrote the stunning, fuguelike last movement of his *Jupiter* Symphony in a few days. Nor was this the only thing that occupied him during the late summer of 1788, even though, with the exception of the *Jupiter*, that period can seem fallow when you place it in the overall context of his career.

VIRTUALLY EVERY major orchestral conductor has recorded at least a few of Mozart's symphonies, with the preponderance of renderings heavily weighted on the last half dozen. Impossible, really, to feel choose among such riches, but also impossible not to feel enthusiastic appreciation for Herbert von Karajan and the Berlin Philharmonic's authoritative, magisterial late 1970s recordings of the final six symphonies, reissued on a double Deutsche Grammophon CD.

Other excellent interpretations of many of these works include recordings by Günter Wand with the NDR Symphony Orchestra, Sir Neville Marriner with the Academy of St. Martin in the Fields, Daniel Barenboim leading the English Chamber Orchestra, and Frans Brüggen and the Orchestra of the Eighteenth Century (so named because the musicians are playing original instruments, or copies, from the eighteenth

or just as a man in such a towering rage oversteps all the bounds of order, moderation and propriety and completely forgets himself, so must the music too forget itself. But since passions, whether violent or not, must never be expressed to the point of exciting disgust, [so] music, even in the most terrible situations, must never offend the ear, but must please the listener, or in other words must never cease to be *music.*"

—Mozart, writing to his father, September 26, 1781

century). Late in his life, Leonard Bernstein returned to Mozart, and his nuanced recordings of the fortieth and the forty-first symphonies are notable for both the extraordinary sound of the Vienna Philharmonic and the occasional liberties Bernstein takes with traditional tempos. A recent recording treat comes from Claudio Abbado leading his Orchestra Mozart in deeply committed, passionate interpretations of several of the later symphonies.

While many of these and other Mozart recordings can be downloaded from iTunes, for the inveterate collector Brilliant has a boxed set of the complete works of Mozart. This uneven, humungous set of 170 CDs includes many recordings by relatively unknown artists, accounting in part for the bargain price online of little more than $100.

Claudio Abbado conducting the London Symphony at the Great Performers series at Lincoln Center, May 2, 1983.

SELECTED SYMPHONIES

No. 27, K. 183

One of the last symphonies he wrote in his youth, Symphony no. 27 in G Major is also one of many Mozart symphonies with only three movements. The movements themselves are also quite short, with the entire piece taking little more than fifteen minutes in a typical performance. What is immediately striking in this relatively straightforward work is the ease

In Concert

Bach plays well even on a synthesizer, but the better the musicians, the better Mozart sounds. Although they perform other repertoire as well, to hear the Freiburg Baroque Orchestra in a live presentation of one of Mozart's great symphonies is an unforgettable experience. This unusual assemblage of players, who run their orchestra in a kind of partnership arrangement, has also recorded—notably, under the baton of René Jacobs— some of Mozart's finest operas. In concert, however, the group often takes one Mozart symphony and splits it up over the course of a program, with the first movement at the start and then, after a different work by Mozart or a piece by someone else, the second movement, and so on. Long before the advent of television, radio, recordings, and music unions, this was a not atypical concert, wherein an audience might be enthralled for much longer than the two hours, plus or minus, that we are used to today.

and confidence with which the seventeen-year-old composer goes about the task. Note the lovely balance of strings and winds in the sprightly first-movement Allegro and the already sophisticated command of counterpoint in the third-movement Presto. You will want to listen to the second-movement Andantino grazioso at least twice. Its lyric, *ländler*-like melody, the kind Mahler would exploit a century later, is notable for its elegance and form. And the understated emotion is a preview of what Mozart will do far more profoundly in the slow movements of such compositions as the piano concertos of the early to mid-1780s.

No. 31, K. 297, *Paris*

Written in the city that gives this symphony its name, the *Paris* Symphony in D Major is also one of the first that Mozart composed as an adult, albeit a young one. Twenty-two years old, he was in Paris in the summer of 1778 with his mother, who died shortly after the first performance of the work.

Not for that reason, but at the request of the conductor, Jean Le Gros, Mozart rewrote the second-movement Andante of the three-movement work, changing the time signature from 6/8 to 3/4. The piece, which was a hit in Paris, makes few major demands on the contemporary listener, for whom the chief historical interest may be that for the first time, a Mozart symphony includes parts for the clarinet (an instrument Mozart would grow to love). Thus, the piece has more of the textured sound we associate with Mozart's mature symphonies; the tuttis (all of

Mozart's mother, Maria Anna. She died when Mozart was twenty-two years old and spending the summer with her in Paris. (Unsigned drawing)

the strings together) in the short, third-movement Allegro especially augment this sense.

No. 35, K. 385, *Haffner*

Listening to the *Haffner* Symphony, written in 1782 when Mozart was twenty-six, we discover a piece that has all the feel and depth of greatness. Mozart composed this symphony for a ceremony honoring a family friend in Salzburg who was being made a noble, but it is unlikely that the occasion itself was the cause of the music's obvious profundity, from the opening chords of the Allegro con spirito first movement.

Since settling in Vienna, marrying, and writing the successful opera *Die Entführung aus dem Serail* (The Abduction from the Seraglio), Mozart was a new man. He had ceremoniously left the employ of Archbishop Colloredo and was in the process of separating himself personally and musically from his father, Leopold. Whether in response to all of this or not, the *Haffner* moves forcefully from the first movement to a lovely, second-movement Andante, notable for the extended, lyrical development. This is the Mozart whose music we want to hear again and again; repetition only increases the pleasure. The short, stately third-movement Minuet is one in which you can almost imagine court figures dancing at a state occasion, while the equally short fourth-movement Presto finale races to its bravura conclusion. The Haffner family had to have been happy, and this piece will leave you feeling that way, too.

*I*f this were a place where people had ears to hear and hearts to feel and if they understood even a little about music and taste, I'd laugh heartily . . . but—as far as music is concerned—I'm among beasts and brutes. But how could it be otherwise, they're exactly the same in all their actions, emotions and passions—there's nowhere in the world like Paris."

—Mozart, writing to his father, May 1, 1778

No. 36, K. 425, *Linz*

Only someone with a very cold heart or tin ears could resist the extended opening of the beautiful

Linz Symphony, written—incredibly—over a long weekend in Linz, where in 1783 Mozart and his new wife, Constanze, had arrived only to learn that an orchestra had been hired and the performance of a symphony was expected. This amazing four-movement work in C major moves into a gorgeous, second-movement Andante that is almost as long as the first movement (more than seven minutes). After a shorter, third-movement Minuet, the fourth-movement Presto again vies for something of a record length so far in Mozart's symphonic oeuvre, setting the standard for the symphonies that followed. The Presto may remind you of something by Beethoven, who was only a boy when it was written; he clearly listened to it as a man.

No. 38, K. 504, *Prague*

The last of Mozart's symphonies to be only three movements, the *Prague* Symphony is in every other way still an extended work; in fact, its first-movement Adagio-allegro clocks in at more than ten minutes. But the grandeur of this symphony, written for a visit that Mozart made in early 1786 to Prague, where his opera *The Marriage of Figaro* was playing to huge acclaim, is hardly measured by its length alone. Just the opening of the first movement, which at a third of the entire movement is longer than the opening of the *Linz*, should be enough to create musical nirvana. And then the actual first theme comes in! Paradise. The Andante, second movement, that follows is heart-breaking—fragile, spare, delicate, sweet, aching. The Presto finale relieves some of the stressful anguish but leaves you wondering which Mozart you are listening to: melancholy or jubilant? The answer is a triumphant both!

No. 39, K. 543

Paradise again, this time for Symphony no. 39, an entire four-movement symphony, the least frequently performed of Mozart's final three but perhaps the most inscrutable. Like the two that followed, written during the summer of 1788, this E-flat-major master-piece is a work to take with you to that proverbial desert isle, if you can take only one. How many ways are there to say *beautiful*? This symphony asks, and asks again, and again. Just the opening several dozen measures, with the ascending scales and the descending arpeggios, are enough to transport most of us to heaven. But there is more! So much more, even in the first-movement Adagio-allegro—such a sweet combination of moods and tempos, just like the first movement of the earlier *Prague* Symphony. Still to come are a stately, delicate Andante second movement, a completely exuberant Minuetto: Allegretto third that leaves everyone on his or her feet, wanting to dance, all capped by an Allegro finale, short like the third movement but swift in its immediate penetration to your suspended sense that the world can actually, truly be a good place. Champagne for everyone!

No. 40, K. 550

Probably the most popular of Mozart's symphonies, with an opening that has even become a cell-phone ringtone, the great Symphony no. 40 in G Minor is, quite simply, music to die for. No one could do this as easily as Mozart—or was its composition more of a struggle than we surmise, given the brief time he spent on it? Who can say? Who can explain its transition from the celebration of that first movement's Molto allegro to the controlled, tense sadness of the second movement's Andante? Do we hear an echo of Mozart's grief over the death that same summer of his infant daughter, Theresia? Again, we cannot say; we can only wonder. Oh, the Minuetto third movement! Relief at last . . . except, what is that we hear in the equally short fourth-movement Allegro assai? A compromise that bridges the gulf between agony and ecstasy? Make of it what you will, there had until its composition never been anything like this symphony in the history of music.

No. 41, K. 551, *Jupiter*

They had to rewrite the textbooks again after the *Jupiter* Symphony. Stupendous. Unbelievable. Beyond superlatives. Maybe simply: miraculous.

This perfect piece, one of the great musical compositions by anyone in the history of Western classical music, takes us on a journey from the inspired to the sublime, with stops along the way at the cheerful and the tragic.

Commentary on this symphony focuses especially on the finale, with its fuguelike organization. The counterpoint here owes a deep debt to the example of J. S. Bach, whose music Mozart studied seriously during the last half-dozen years of his life. But the power of this movement depends as much on Mozart's marshaling of the full orchestra's resources, giving us the sense of a nineteenth-century sound.

The thrill to the listener of much of that fourth movement's energy is based on the contrast with what has preceded it, particularly in the sighs of the second-movement Andante cantabile. The repeated figure here, its rhythm mimicking a heartbeat, must be one of the single most beautiful moments in all of Mozart's music.

Concertante

Consider a rose garden in Mozart's Vienna, the petals cut and the stems trimmed back because late autumn will soon yield to winter. Gone are the leaves on all of the trees in the beautiful park at the city's center. Somewhere a gentle waterfall feeds a small pond, the water's rush making a sound that syncopates with the clatter of horses' hooves on a nearby street. Dawn has ushered in another day in the lives of the city's people, who include a congenitally busy composer named Mozart. He grew up, when he wasn't traveling, in a different, smaller city, where he can remember a river set against a small mountain, perhaps in the mist. By what pathway did he get from "there" to "here"?

If, so far as we know from his letters, Mozart rarely posed such questions in his daily life, he was constantly doing so in his music. Everything he wrote had something to do with motion, going "somewhere," and the path—the particular piece of music he was writing at a given time—took varied forms but always grew out of Mozart's relationship to, his place in, a particular moment.

Copycats

Beyond the triple phenomenon of creativity, talent, and concentration, for Mozart composing also represented physical labor. All of those notes! To get them down on paper—just the actual process of doing so, moving one's arms, holding the pen, sitting still for hours at a time—was no easy task. And then, when Mozart had completed a piece, unless it was for solo instrument alone—say, a piano sonata—there was the additional chore of copying out the parts for each of the different instrumentalists.

By the time he was married and living in Vienna, Mozart employed what until just recently in music history (with the advent of the computer) were an essential tool of the trade: copyists. These individuals, usually skilled musicians with a good hand, performed the laborious task of breaking down a full score and painstakingly copying out what the first violins were to play, then the second violins, the violas, the cellos, and so on. The job was made more challenging because even a composer of Mozart's stature could make mistakes, and a trained copyist needed to be able to spot them.

But, in Mozart's perhaps unique case, there was a further concern, especially after the enormous popular and critical success of the first of Mozart's greatest operas, *The Marriage of Figaro*, in 1785. What if a copyist working on the parts of, say, a new Mozart symphony, made an extra copy for himself?

To keep an eye on everyone—to be sure each copyist was not only working but also not stealing—the Mozarts often had the copyists come to their home, where Constanze could watch over them while her husband continued to create.

And so, not the least of the astonishments Mozart left us in his music are the constant reminders that each day matters. Though, of course, not everything he composed is a masterpiece, he never did things by rote. This is especially amazing when you consider the sheer size of his nonsymphonic orchestral output, which includes pieces classified as concertante, meaning they are symphonic in form but give prominence to a solo instrument or two within the orchestra.

With the caveat that there can be confusion in some cases about which pieces to place in the broad, nonsymphonic orchestral category, there is no denying that Mozart wrote a tremendous amount of them. Moreover, so much of Mozart's oeuvre is orchestra-based that one would stand on firm ground making the argument that many of his concertos could have been symphonies, and many of his symphonies, with the addition of a piano or another solo instrument, could have been concertos.

Even safely within the nonsymphonic orchestral category, what constitutes a Mozart orchestra is open to interpretation. He wrote several serenades, including at least one that no one else ever topped, the Serenade in B-flat, K. 361, nicknamed *Gran Partita*, and a cross between a serenade and a divertimento, *Eine kleine Nachtmusik* (A Little Night Music), K. 525. Both are scored for only partial orchestra, the former for wind instruments and double bass, the latter for strings only.

He wrote divertimentos. Minuets. Short pieces he called "German Dances." Numerous orchestral works for solo voice and various orchestralike combinations of instruments and more than one singer.

He composed at least two masterpieces for orchestra in which certain instruments are given solo prominence. Concertone, K. 186, an early hit, is scored for two violins and orchestra, while the later Sinfonia Concertante, K. 364, features both a solo violin and a solo viola with orchestra.

All of these works exude a luxury of harmony, both in the structure of the written lines and in the combination of the instruments themselves. In the Andante of the *Gran Partita*, for example, the music more than once seems ready to soar right out of whatever room in which you are lucky enough to be listening to it.

SUCH A RECORDED WEALTH FROM WHICH to choose here, but few recordings of the *Gran Partita* can be more beautiful than that of the Orpheus Chamber Orchestra, in a Deutsche Grammophon disc that pairs the piece with the Serenade in E-flat. And could two string players be better matched than violinist Itzhak Perlman and violist Pinchas Zuckerman in the Sinfonia Concertante, again on a DG disc? Zubin Mehta

Itzhak Perlman and Gerard Schwarz at a rehearsal for Mostly Mozart,
July 12, 1989.

leads the Israel Philharmonic Orchestra on a classic
recording that also includes the Concertone, again with
Perlman and Zuckerman, both playing the violin. There
may be more recordings of *Eine kleine Nachtmusik*
than even the most inveterate of collectors can own,
but a superb choice is the reissue on Naxos of Wilhelm
Furtwängler's historic 1949 recording with the Vienna
Philharmonic Orchestra.

SELECTED CONCERTANTE

Concertone, K. 190

A youthful piece that only someone very talented could
have written at whatever age, Concertone is something
of a three-movement symphony crossed with a violin

The Joke's on Me

The same year—1787—that Mozart wrote some of his most exalted compositions, including what is arguably his finest opera, *Don Giovanni,* he also composed a send-up of musical incompetence and philistine tendentiousness. Called *Ein musikalischer Spass* (A Musical Joke), K. 522, the piece is at once hilarious in its structured effect and profound in its implicit commentary. "Don't take yourself too seriously," Mozart seems to be saying, even as by other examples he all but says that everything in life matters. Especially delightful is the work's conclusion, a cacophony of musical malapropisms that portends the most extreme licenses taken by the so-called avant-garde two centuries later. Among a miscellany of Mozartiana that includes arrangements of music by other composers, notably a onetime Mozart mentor, C. P. E. Bach, *A Musical Joke* stands sui generis.

concerto—except here there are two solo violins, rather than just one. Although the entire work is melodic, it does not contain the kind of mature Mozart tune that you find yourself hearing over and over in your head after a performance or a recording. Listen, however, to the relative sophistication with which Mozart wrote for his small orchestra here, and note how seamlessly he integrated the two violins, in a manner that would later become a kind of trademark. Enjoy the innocence of the harmony, a far cry from, say, that of *Don Giovanni*, which was still almost fifteen years away.

Serenade in B-flat, K. 361, *Gran Partita*

Gran Partita is a certifiable masterpiece, one of Mozart's first. This breakthrough composition for a dozen wind instruments and double bass still sounds ahead of its time, more than two hundred years after it was written. Wind ensembles were popular in Mozart's day, but what we find here is a new sense of their possibilities, combined with a clear, confident lyrical grasp of the serenade's form. From the very first ensemble chord, this seven-section work startles us to attention, and its third-section Adagio is simply a rapture. Throughout this serenade, it is as if we are listening in on Mozart as he experiments with different wind sonorities that he will go on to use to such grand effect in his full orchestral writing.

Sinfonia Concertante, K. 364

Another early masterpiece, which was actually written before Concertone, despite its slightly later Köchel number, Mozart's Sinfonia Concertante is again in the form of a three-movement symphony, this time with prominence given to a solo violin and a solo viola. Perhaps because Mozart especially loved the viola, which he later exploited in his string quintets, there is a quality of affection that runs throughout this work, sentimental though it may seem to say this. After a gorgeous opening Allegro maestoso, in which the pattern of musical conversation between the violin and the viola is set, the piece goes into an altogether higher gear in the deeply felt, second-movement Andante. The third movement, marked Presto, is exuberant, a buoyant feel-good moment in Mozart's oeuvre.

Eine kleine Nachtmusik, K. 525

A relatively late work in Mozart's career and certainly one of the most recognizable, *Eine kleine Nachtmusik* is a four-movement crowd-pleaser scored for strings only. Again, Mozart gets right to it, with a strongly accented opening sequence that sets not only the tone but the feeling of this entire piece. Listen afterward to one of the symphonies Mozart wrote around this time in his life (the late 1780s) and marvel at how he was able to achieve such transparency with his strings, whether with or without winds. Tchaikovsky did it once without winds, but one searches for another example of a composer who pulled this off again until Stravinsky.

Concertos for Strings and Winds

Although Mozart was best known during his lifetime for his virtuosity on the piano, he also played—sometimes in public—the violin. Perhaps because of this expansive background and skill, Mozart excelled at writing concertos for violin, which in a general sense differed from their concertante siblings due to the further prominence given to the solo instrument. Within the same idea of "almost concertante," Mozart also composed a number of wonderful concertos for wind instruments, including a clarinet concerto that may be the finest piece featuring that instrument by anyone.

All told, in addition to the clarinet masterpiece, Mozart wrote five concertos for violin, plus two rondos and two single-movement works. He also wrote four concertos for horn, two for flute (plus an andante and a concerto for flute and harp), and both an oboe concerto and a bassoon concerto (one of few in the entire literature). Much of his concerto work came early to midway in his career, although the clarinet concerto, K. 622, with a ravishingly beautiful slow movement, was one of the last pieces of music he ever composed.

Refined Grace

For Amnon Levy, longtime Boston Symphony Orchestra first violinist, Mozart's music is nothing short of "amazing," in part because "Mozart packed so much of it into such a short life." Ironically, Mozart's piano concertos are among Levy's favorite works, "because the orchestra is not an accompaniment. Mozart put a lot into them, more than in his violin concertos. And in his sonatas for violin and piano, the piano is more important." Levy, seventy-seven, began playing in the orchestra in 1964 and is retiring at the end of the 2009 summer season in Tanglewood. During his distinguished career, he has played in countless performances of Mozart's works and is always struck by how graciously Mozart wrote for his instrument, the violin. "You have to live and feel that way," Levy says, "more so than with any other composer, even Beethoven. It takes a lot of time to develop this refined grace, to be able to project that quality in your playing. Many people can play the notes but they might sound crudely. You have to seek with Mozart, have in your mind the sound you are looking for, and eventually you get it."

All of these compositions share a Mozartean trait in which the solo instrument, while of course foremost, is never left exposed for the simple purpose of showing off. The solo instrument in a Mozart concerto, in other words, plays *with* the orchestra. Even in a cadenza (an improvised passage in which only the solo instrument performs) the crucial Mozart aesthetic, as always, is to create a unity of purpose, a commonality of expression within whatever form a particular piece has taken. This is a huge difference from many of the concertos that followed in the nineteenth century, when the musical conception—the piece itself—is often overwhelmed by the demanding pyrotechnics required of the soloist. One thinks, for example, of the piano concertos of Chopin, which, lacking the integration of the orchestra, would probably have been long forgotten were it not for the fireworks in the pianist's part.

There came a time in Mozart's career when he chafed at the demands of continuing to play the violin. "Again, you say—'*I will no longer be a fiddler*,'" Leopold Mozart (himself a violinist) wrote to his son in the fall of 1778. "Why, formerly, you were nothing but a fiddler.... As a lover of music you will not consider it beneath you to play the violin in the first symphony...You would surely not deny to Haydn certain achievements in music? Has he, a Konzertmeister, become a court viola-player, because he plays that instrument in the chamber music concerts? Why, one does it for one's own amusement; and as the concert is short and only consists of four items, believe me that to play is a pleasant recreation as one doesn't know what to do with oneself in the evenings."

Indeed. Behind his father's remonstrance lies an important point, which Leopold makes deprecatingly in his use of the word *entertainment*. No harm in sending concertgoers home happy—which is what most of these concertos do. Or, depending on the programming, they set the stage, often opening a concert as an appetizer or, following a brief work, just before intermission. Most of them are relatively short themselves, although they are by no means a snap to play.

Although Mozart was best known as a piano virtuoso, he sometimes also performed on the violin, which he had basically taught himself to play as a child. (C. 1894)

According to the great violinist Jascha Heifetz, "On the whole, Mozart's writing is very violinistic, but it is never easy to play." Heifetz, who apocryphally responded once to a fan's praise after a performance with the retort, "How would you know?" was a stern judge. "You must play [Mozart's] music as written without adding any outside interpretation," he explained. "The pieces that look, or even sound easy, are the really hard ones. There must be sentiment without sentimentality."

This last was a remark that would have especially pleased Mozart, who eschewed cheap tricks for forced tears in everything he wrote or played. The composer was a soft touch, but he never exploited personal feelings in his music for the sake of a fake emotion. And in person, you still had to earn his affection. But once you did . . . if you were a musician, he might write you a concerto, which is exactly what prompted such works as the Clarinet Concerto. He composed it in 1791 for his good friend Anton Stadler, a virtuoso extraordinaire, whom Mozart had known since the early 1780s. Mozart scored his Clarinet Concerto for an instrument called a basso clarinet, which has the range of a modern clarinet in the key of A.

YOU CAN'T GO WRONG WITH THE NAXOS reissue of Dennis Brain's great 1954 recordings as soloist in the horn concertos, while James Galway's rapturous playing remains a benchmark in the flute concertos, on an RCA recording that also includes Galway and harpist Marisa Robles in the flute and harp concerto.

For the violin concertos, a wonderfully nuanced two-disc Philips reissue of recordings made in the 1960s features Arthur Grumiaux. Most of the music, which includes one of the rondos, K. 373; the Adagio in E, K. 261; and the Sinfonia Concertante (with the addition of violist Arrigo Pellicia) is under the baton of Sir Colin Davis, leading the London Symphony Orchestra. Raymond Leppard and the New Philharmonia Orchestra contribute the Adagio and the Rondo.

If you are searching for a good recording of the Clarinet Concerto, any of several recordings with either Gervase de Peyer or Sabine. Meyer as soloist are fine choices.

Sir James Galway and his "magic" golden flute.

SELECTED CONCERTOS FOR STRINGS AND WINDS

Violin Concertos nos. 1 through 5, K. 207, 211, 216, 218, and 219

The optimistic violin concertos nos. 1 through 5, all composed when Mozart was still an adolescent (but not, as long thought, all within months of one another), brim with young vigor and élan. They are also much more difficult to play than they sound. The best known is the third, in G major; its second-movement Adagio contains what is surely one of Mozart's best-loved melodies. Could the person who wrote this really have been only sixteen? Listen to the slow movement of the fourth concerto too, and Mozart's lyrical feeling for this instrument is doubly apparent.

Clarinet Concerto in A Major, K. 622

Once Mozart discovered the clarinet, he could not get enough of it, sometimes including it in a symphonic score in place of the oboe and writing chamber music for it as well, notably the Clarinet Quintet in A, K. 581. This deeply expressive work, with an Adagio second movement that stands among Mozart's finest creations, is arguably the best piece ever written for this talismanic instrument.

Flute Concertos 1 and 2, K. 313 and K. 314
Horn Concertos 1 through 4, K. 412/514, 417, 447, and 495

Except for the trumpet, for which his father, Leopold, wrote a concerto that is still performed today, Mozart composed concertos for all of the major wind instruments of his era, including even the oboe and the bassoon. He also wrote a lovely concerto for flute and harp, K. 299. His two flute concertos and the later series of horn concertos are all notable for the same uncanny ensemble ideal that Mozart displayed at its greatest height in his piano concertos. Choose any from the list, and you will immediately find striking the way in which Mozart is able to exploit the intrinsic qualities of whatever solo instrument he has chosen for a particular concerto, but always with the higher motive of everything for the music's sake.

MUSINGS ON

Sir James Galway on Playing Mozart

Mozart's music is not difficult to play. In fact, most professional musicians can handle it technically. The difficulty with Mozart is to play with the charm and virtuosity required. In playing Mozart ones tries to recapture the expression of the age.

Chamber Music

"A father, having decided to send his children out into the wide world, felt that he should entrust them to the protection and guidance of a famous Man who by good fortune also was his best Friend," Mozart wrote to the older composer Franz Joseph Haydn on September 1, 1785. The occasion was the completion and dedication (to Haydn) of six string quartets, the first of which, K. 387, Mozart had started to sketch two years earlier. "They are, to be truthful, the fruit of long and laborious efforts," Mozart continued, in a confession that was as rare as it was also, in this case, true.

Remarkably, the same composer who wrote his last three symphonies in a single stretch of only a few months found the composition of the six Haydn string quartets a greater challenge. What emerged in the music, however, is something that belies that struggle. From the very opening of K. 387, with its buoyant, transparent melody, the listener is rewarded with a piece that brims with rhythmic and contrapuntal invention, creating a quartet sound that is as fresh now as it was innovative then—so full and deep that it is often impossible to believe that only four instruments are playing.

Someone wondering what Mozart's music is about could do worse than to begin with this quartet. On a first hearing, the music can seem a little unapproachable, if only because it appears to be so different from the magnificent symphonies, the memorable concertos, and the stunning operas. Given the small ensemble—in the case of a quartet: two violins, a viola, and a cello—it can also strike the uninitiated as Mozart in miniature. But Mozart's chamber music, which includes a panorama of other quartets, unparalleled string quintets

Festivals and Feasts

So much music, so little time . . . but if you happen to be in Vermont some summer weekend between mid-July and mid-August, the famed Marlboro Music Festival takes place every Saturday evening and Sunday afternoon, with an occasional Friday evening as well. Started more than fifty years ago by pianist Rudolf Serkin, flutist Marcel Moyse, and others, the festival is directed now by two preeminent Mozart performers, pianists Richard Goode and Mitsuko Uchida. Programs of chamber music are never announced ahead of time, but some will invariably include a work or two of Mozart's, perhaps even one played by Serkin's son, Peter, also a pianist and a notable interpreter of Mozart. And there cannot be a more beautiful place to hear such music; Marlboro is a tiny town nestled in the Green Mountains in the southernmost part of the state.

(with two violas), and numerous other combinations (several featuring the piano), is an entire, enormous sonic world.

What, then, is its "subject"? The question has vexed musicians and audiences alike, even as the music has beguiled, entranced, stirred, and calmed them. Impossible, of course, to say exactly, but that is both the charm and the challenge. But perhaps to search for the right answer is to ask a different question: what was it—is it—in this chamber music that draws us? What is the source of its power? And this question about Mozart is not a puzzle but the very thread of the entire fabric, to mix a metaphor. Mozart's impact in human terms is that great.

In part because its architecture is so clearly defined, the chamber music is an excellent place to reflect on this question and probe, if not for answers, then for hints, intimations, even revelations. Nor is this the purview of the esoteric. As in so many walks of life, the devil is in the details.

Within the rather large and to some extent loosely defined musical genre of chamber music—music that was originally composed to be played by a few musicians for their own pleasure in a room—Mozart also wrote duos and trios for strings, a couple of sonatas for strings, many works for violin and piano (including two superb piano quartets: string trio plus piano), and several quartets and quintets for various combinations of strings and wind instruments.

In most of these compositions, Mozart's debt to Bach is immediately apparent. This is particularly the case in the later works with regard to Mozart's use of counterpoint (the relationship of one instrument's melodic line to another's). And in his quartets, Mozart is clearly inspired by the example set by Haydn in taking a form that had often been merely a divertissement and making it into a highly ordered work of art.

Listen, for starters, to the beautiful second movement of the String Quartet in E-flat, K. 428, the third composed (and the fourth in the first edition) of the quartets that Mozart dedicated so fulsomely to Haydn. Observe, first of all, how nothing in this Andante con moto is there simply for décor—even though *everything* is "decorative," but in the sense of enhancing the loveliness of melody and harmony. Note as well the grace with which the four instruments trade the melodic line; even the cello (the instrument with the lowest range in a string quartet) carries the "tune" at times. Hear the way Mozart employs a mix of phrasing to accentuate the forward-feeling motion of the 6/8 meter (six beats to a measure, with an eighth note receiving a beat). Within that thrust, sense the strong emotion of longing that drives or dominates this entire section of the quartet. Cross that longing with something in your own life—missing a friend, saying good-bye to a close relative—and grasp that the person who wrote this extraordinary music in 1783 was not yet thirty years old.

THE GOLD STANDARD IN RECORDINGS of the *Haydn* Quartets are those by the venerable Budapest String Quartet, on a set of CDs reissued by Sony. But there are numerous others to choose from, including those by the Tallich Quartet and the Alban Berg Quartett. The Tallich Quartet, augmented by violist Karel Rehak, has also recorded a highly prized interpretation of the complete string quintets. But it would be difficult to find the equal of the 1967 recordings by the Grumiaux Quartett with Georges Janzer as the additional violist. Reissued in an inexpensive CD format by Philips, these discs boast warmth, authority, and drop-dead virtuosity. A bonus on the third disc is the Divertimento in E-flat Major, K. 563, but you will want to spend extra listening time with the fifth and the sixth of the quintets, particularly the inspiring slow movements.

For the uninitiated and the expert alike, one would have to look a long time to find a better recorded introduction to Mozart's chamber music than the Sony Legacy reissue of hall-of-fame producer Steve Epstein's CD of Mozart's two piano quartets. The all-star quartet is composed of Emanuel Ax, piano; Isaac Stern, violin; Jaime Laredo, viola; and Yo-Yo Ma, cello. Simply the first two minutes of the second of these quartets, K. 493, ought to be enough to cure anyone of the blues.

Yo-Yo Ma in rehearsal for the Great Performers series at Lincoln Center, May 3, 1985.

SELECTED CHAMBER MUSIC

Haydn Quartets, K. 387, 421, 428,
458, 464, and 465

For a person who loves Mozart or is just becoming acquainted with him, but who is at least a little intimidated by his chamber music—or by anyone's—the *Haydn* Quartets are a good place to start. Written over the course of two years in the 1780s, they are framed by four other quartets, with which they are often grouped as the "ten celebrated string quartets." One of those others, the String Quartet in B-flat, K. 465, nicknamed *The Hunt*, is also an excellent choice as a starting point for a newcomer, whereas veteran Mozartphiles can get a daily chamber music fix with one of the dozens of other chamber music combinations Mozart tried (numerous trios, for example, some for strings alone and others for two string players and piano). In whatever capacity you come to the *Haydn* Quartets, three main aspects will immediately engage you: their lyrical beauty, the intricacy of their form, and the ways in which you can hear Mozart developing the same conversational quality that defines the scoring of his mature symphonies and operas. In part by emulating the innovations of Franz Joseph Haydn, Mozart in these works dispenses with the old formulaic model of theme and variations and lets his instrumentalists respond to one another. In this regard, you might even think of these quartets as being a little like jazz, although with the major caveat, of course, that the "improvisation" has been written out beforehand by Mozart.

String Quintets, K. 174, 406, 515, 516, 593, and 614

These extraordinary string quintets, all but one written in Mozart's maturity and the last written near the end of his life, take what Mozart accomplished in his finest string quartets and exponentially enlarge it. Imagine, for example, that you were playing full-court, pickup basketball with four players to a side. Suddenly, two more players show up and you add one of them to each of your two teams. Now, the player who was previously the lone guard and therefore focused mostly on defense can use more of the court, pass the ball, and even shoot instead of hanging back, because he or she has help. And the analogy goes further: the five-person team can try all sorts of plays that would have been impossible with four. The same applies to a string quintet: with the addition of a second violist to the traditional string quartet, Mozart here is able, literally, to *play* with both the form *and* the parts. Dip into one of these quintets almost anywhere and you will hear a highly refined intelligence pushing the boundaries of normal expectation. You will hear complex counterpoint in both K. 593's and K. 614's last movements, gorgeous melody in movement after movement—start with the soaring second-movement Andante of K. 506—and instrumental part writing that explores, say, a cellist's ability to take the melody or a violinist's the harmony. Especially interesting here, with the two violas and the dark sound of that instrument Mozart so loved, are the repeated moments of interlocking and releasing as the part of one crosses with that of the other, then comes together before splitting again but in a different direction. Come to think of it, you could add that idea to the repertoire of the Celtics or the Lakers.

Piano Quartets nos. 1 and 2, K. 478 and K. 493

It should come as no surprise that musicians love to play the Piano Quartets nos. 1 and 2, or the enormous number of other compositions that Mozart wrote for piano and string players. They are, for the musician, not only challenging but fun, and you will feel this way as a listener, too. The addition of the piano to the small ensemble somehow removes any remaining modern stigma of "serious" that the term *chamber music* still carries for many of us. Mozart, of course, always took what he was doing seriously, insofar as he never dumbed down the music. But for him, the opportunity to write and perform this music was first and foremost a pleasure; the *reason*, if you will, that he made the sacrifices he did. The glorious sense that as he composed these quartets the last thing on his mind was "doing his job" comes across thrillingly in the energetic opening of K. 493 and then simply melts any last defenses you may have in the same work's second-movement Larghetto. The piano takes the lead there, as it does in the third-movement Rondo that concludes K. 478, but every instrument has an equal role to play—yet another way in which this music resembles jazz in its democratic allocation of means toward a common end. Enjoy!

Vocal Music

The truth, as the old saying goes, will set you free. Although, as far as we know, it was not a mantra known to Mozart, his music for voice surely bears it out.

You could argue that everything Mozart wrote was a kind of song, and you'd be on pretty firm ground. The only caveat you'd have to make, of course, is that in much of his music, the part for the human voice has been given to a solo instrument or, in the case of such orchestral works as his symphonies, a whole section of instruments. But again and again, in piece after piece, whatever Mozart composed *sings*. The "tune," as he heard it, is the truth as he experienced it, felt it, believed it.

Except perhaps in some of his operas (discussed, along with his songs and concert arias, in the Opera section beginning on page 139) and in his sacred music, as we shall see here, Mozart never declared in words what the truth was or is. Even in an operatic or other text, you can never be sure what he was thinking. Mozart was too circumspect and equivocal to make bald, didactic pronouncements. His letters as well, for all their newsiness and gossip, contain very little existential or metaphysical reflection. The music itself is the only reliable guide.

All told, Mozart wrote more than a hundred compositions that fall under the umbrella of nonoperatic vocal

Piano Lessons

Throughout most of his adult life, Mozart was obliged to take on pupils as a source of income. Occasionally, one of them proved adept as a composer, most notably Franz Xaver Süssmayr, who was with Mozart when he died and who at Constanze's request completed a version of the unfinished Requiem. Another was a British man, Thomas Attwood, who went on to a long and successful career as an organist.

Attwood is notable as well because he kept a record of his lessons, which took place during the period in early 1786 when Mozart was completing and then presenting his opera *The Marriage of Figaro*. Emerging from his portrait of Mozart is a teacher of rigorous standards, who drilled Attwood in methodical counterpoint exercises. Mozart the teacher did not give out gold stars for trying; he expected a student to work hard, and he took his teaching seriously. Attwood's notebooks are filled with corrections and suggestions from the master. It was a method that Mozart himself learned and relearned from his father.

"Nothing can be done without toil!" Leopold reminded his son in a long letter in 1778. "If some things don't turn out as you want, hope or imagine . . . remember that it has always been like this in the world."

music. They range from several ensemble pieces for voice and piano or other instruments to numerous short canons, from a few oratorios to a string of church sonatas (like much of the sacred music, composed in Mozart's adolescence in Salzburg). But the heart of this part of his oeuvre are two fine masses, a number of masterful shorter sacred works that defy specific categorization, and the unfinished Requiem.

In all of these pieces and despite the repeated avowals of faith in his letters (particularly with regard to the occasion of someone's death), Mozart comes across as what the late theologian Reinhold Niebuhr might have called a devout skeptic. Mozart rarely fails to give stated credence to an expression of religious piety. But the impression that the music gives makes one wonder. The contrast with Bach, for example, is striking; little equivocation seems apparent in Bach's Mass in B Minor and the *Saint Matthew Passion*. Bach is a believer. On the other hand, Mozart wants to be a believer, thinks he ought to be, or once almost was. But the music reigns supreme, being itself, to paraphrase Thornton Wilder's description of love at the conclusion of his short novel *The Bridge of San Luis Rey*, the bridge to Mozart's belief, the only survival and the only meaning.

Masses

Many of Mozart's masses survive only in part or were never finished in the first place. Others, notably the Coronation Mass, K. 317, written near the end of Mozart's unhappy Salzburg period under Archbishop Colloredo, adopted the then popular form of a *missa brevis*, a mass in which the Credo is missing. Many of his masses, in fact, carried that appellation and many would no longer be heard today were they not composed by

Mozart. Listening to them is often an exercise in musical biography, as if their very brevity and relative commonality were a musical metaphor for Mozart's increasing exasperation in the service of the archbishop, for his chafing at what he came to regard more or less as indentured servitude.

Indisputably, the landmark work in Mozart's composition of masses is the incomplete Mass in C Minor, K. 427, which Mozart began in 1782 and presented the following year in Salzburg. The occasion, his last visit to the city of his birth, was the introduction of his wife, Constanze, to Leopold, who had opposed the marriage, as he had any of his son's relationships with women. By whatever reasoning, Leopold seemed to believe that his son's focus on music would be impacted negatively by

Politics and Faith

If Mozart's religious faith came forward in his early ecclesiastical works, we would do well to consider that he might have simply been doing his job—which in many of those early cases meant obeying his father. Later works, such as the incomplete Mass in C and the unfinished Requiem, follow the order of religious format but give no real hints of Mozart's personal beliefs. Neither, really, does *The Magic Flute*, insofar as it is concerned in part with principles of the Masons, which Mozart had joined in the mid-1780s, perhaps as a social convenience. He made friends among the Masons, including

Michael Puchberg, from whom he solicited loans, and his librettist on *The Magic Flute*, Emanuel Schikaneder. But did Mozart fully subscribe to the dictums and rituals of the order? It is impossible to say.

As it also is of his political beliefs. Much of his greatest music was written as the American Revolution was taking place, and the French Revolution was still under way during Mozart's last year. Yet there is not a single reference in his correspondence to either of these hugely important historical events. Some commentators have attempted to interpret Don Giovanni's behavior partially in political terms, but Mozart certainly never said as much. It seems more likely that in his brief, busy life he was too preoccupied with his music to partake of politics. And yet, today, were anyone to put him up as a champion of some sort, it would certainly be with a cry of liberty for all. His music is too driven by a deeply felt humanism to be anything else.

romance, whereas all of the evidence in Mozart's music suggests the opposite.

Whatever the inspiration, the Mass in C Minor is a breathtaking piece, building in a sequence of emotional peaks and valleys that in many ways mirror the unfinished Requiem to come. The choral writing is noteworthy not only for the beauty of the harmony but for Mozart's characteristic blending of instrument and voice, wherein the orchestra never indulges in mere accompaniment. Chorus, soloists, and orchestra are full partners.

SELECTED MASSES

Coronation Mass, K. 317

Almost everything Mozart wrote had a kind of vocal quality to it; even the purely instrumental works, whether for small or large ensemble, *sing*. And much of what he wrote was, of course, for singers, most notably opera (and the attendant secular forms of concert aria and song), but a great deal of that output was for the church or with some kind of religious connotation. Growing up, when Mozart wasn't touring, and then as a young adult when he was still living in Salzburg, he wrote a large number of *missae breves* and other so-called sacred works, usually out of a sense of familial, if not religious, duty. One of the best of these, and also one of the last, is the Coronation Mass, K. 317. The mass gets its name from a Prague performance conducted by Mozart's rival Salieri in 1791, twelve years after its composition. The occasion was the coronation of Leopold II, the same event that triggered a commission for what turned out to be Mozart's last opera, *La clemenza di Tito* (The Clemency of Titus). Even in these works, there are bursts of originality and passion that immediately identify their creator. Surely, the soprano solo in the Agnus Dei of the Coronation Mass is such a moment, or that same work's beautiful Benedictus, with its singing strings inviting the soloists, then the full orchestra, and finally the chorus in a great exclamation of blessing.

Mass in C Minor, K. 427

You needn't be a true believer to believe in the goodness and greatness of this beautiful music. Right from the thrilling, opening choral Kyrie, Mozart will hook you; only a cold heart could turn away from this piece, which Mozart wrote soon after finally settling in Vienna. He never quite finished it, but that hardly matters. Listen, for example, to the third section, Laudamus te, which begins with an orchestral figure that may remind you of a passage of Bach's, before the soprano soloist comes in with more than a hint of the vocal calisthenics Mozart will put his beloved sopranos through in his later operas. The piece jumps around a good deal, perhaps the result of the inconclusiveness of its composition, but then it gives us such excesses of beauty as the Qui tollis, an amazing section in which Mozart splits the chorus in two, with each half still having four parts. Magnificent!

Other Choral Works

By the time Mozart composed the Mass in C Minor, the paper trail of letters had begun to thin, so it is now an even greater challenge to decipher the psychology, not to mention the basic chronology, of his creativity. Before he returned to Vienna with Constanze (a fine singer, who was a soloist in the Salzburg performance of the C-minor mass), the Mozarts learned that an infant son they had left in someone else's care in Vienna had died. And yet, on the trip back, they stopped in Linz, where Mozart wrote the *Linz* Symphony, K. 425, over a weekend after his host announced that he had hired an orchestra for the occasion. Who can explain such a phenomenon? Perhaps, as so often seems the case for Mozart, his music was a refuge, as it is centuries later for us—not an escape, but a place that is very much of the world, its pains and losses, yet also its triumphs and loves.

A multitude of other choral music attests to this, beginning with the youthful *Exsultate, jubilate*, K. 165, completed and first performed (in early January 1773) a couple of weeks before Mozart's seventeenth birthday. It is fashionable among Mozart cognoscenti to cite his ninth piano concerto, K. 271, which he composed four years later in 1777, as the moment when Mozart truly began to sound like Mozart. But you'd have a hard time convincing someone hearing the soaring soprano in *Exsultate* that Mozart wasn't already on his game. The piece may not be as subtle as what would follow in such growing complexity and dexterity, but it has more than enough power to stand on its own.

So, too, do such other choral amazements as the Vespers, K. 339, which Mozart composed in 1779, nearing the end of his Salzburg servitude. Could there be five minutes of music more solemnly, lyrically moving than the soprano solo, Laudate Dominum? With the simplest

The Human Voice

Though he was a largely self-taught violinist and violist and a virtuoso pianist, Mozart could also sing, and during the last decade of his life he was married to a singer. What he wrote for the human voice is often extremely difficult to sing; this is especially the case with some of the coloratura soprano arias in his operas. Yet Mozart not only understood but also loved his singers. He sometimes wrote an entire new aria for a particular singer, substituting new for old, when one production included a different cast member than a previous one and the original aria was beyond the technical means of the later singer.

Not every singer through the ages has appreciated this—Maria Callas famously called Mozart's music "dull"—but someone listening to Mozart's writing for the human voice must immediately be struck by how natural it all seems. Unlike the big moments in many of our most popular operas or the vocal solos and choral episodes in, say, Mahler's Second Symphony or Berlioz's Requiem, there is no sense in Mozart of an invisible backstage hand preparing us for what is about to come. No gimmickry, in other words.

For Mozart, the human voice is truly an instrument, as opposed to a stage effect. In the magical *Ave verum corpus*, K. 618—one of the last pieces Mozart ever wrote—for supreme example, the singing simply "appears," a kind of heavenly sonic apparition. Our sense of the singing's purpose is completely grounded in our acceptance of the composition's inevitability. And so, listening, we do not count the measures until something unusual or exciting happens. Rather, we realize that everything in the piece is *of* a piece, singers and orchestra neither yin nor yang, every note whether from voice or player an essential, connected element of the music as a whole. *Whole*: a good word to describe Mozart's conception of the human voice, related as well to its near homonym, *holy*.

of melodies here, at times simply chromatic, and an integration with chorus and orchestra that again comes across as inseparable, Mozart takes us within himself, within the embrace of this music, as if its tensile strength were capable of holding grief, a wrong borne or suffered by the person fortunate enough to encounter its grace.

Requiem, K. 626

By now, the legendary story of Mozart's composing this final, unfinished work as if he were writing music for his own death has been disproved. Yes, he was commissioned to create the work by a stranger, who was doing the bidding of someone else. But we not only know for whom the piece was commissioned—Count Franz von Walsegg-Stuppach, whose wife had recently died—we also understand, after much musicological research, that Mozart knew, too. Nor, until near the very end, did Mozart think he was about to die.

In fact, the period in Mozart's life of the Requiem's composition was among his most busy and fertile, if it is possible to make such fine distinctions in a lifetime of such unparalleled musical labor and creativity. Around the time of the commission he was also asked to write an opera, *La clemenza di Tito*, to commemorate the coronation of Leopold II, who in Prague was ascending to the throne of what was then Hungary and Bohemia. And he was well along in the composition of his last great opera, *The Magic Flute*, which had its Vienna premiere to great acclaim on September 30, 1791 (little more than two months before Mozart's death). In fact, so healthy did Mozart feel until late November that he went to see *The Magic Flute* almost every night it was performed that fall, usually taking a friend with him to share his pleasure.

And in addition to finding time to compose *Ave verum corpus*, he also wrote his great Concerto for Clarinet, K. 622, and the Masonic Cantata, K. 623, which extended the thematic material of *The Magic Flute* (and which may have been inspired by the same impulse that produced the earlier, nonsymphonic orchestral work, his Masonic Funeral Music, K. 477).

Confusion, rather than legend, also characterizes the different versions of the Requiem that now exist. Mozart's widow, Constanze, was left after Mozart's death

Mozart. (Engraving by T. Johnson after a painting by Lorenz)

on December 5, 1791, with many bills and initially little cash and thus was in something of a frenzy to get the piece done. At first, a musician named Joseph Eybler attempted to put the parts together with augmentations of his own. When that failed, Mozart's pupil Franz Xaver Süssmayr stepped in. The version of the Requiem that is usually performed today is the one that Süssmayr, with no lack of skill and a clearly abundant affection for his dead teacher, completed.

Or was Süssmayr motivated by a darker ambition? It's hard to tell, but scholars have long debated not only the relative success of his contributions but also their extent, a process that has been complicated by the claims Süssmayr himself made at the time. In our modern era, more than one musician has tried to unravel what was and wasn't Mozart's original work and intention. What came out of Franz Beyer's 1971 efforts in this regard has been judged by many to be the most successful, yet the debate continues. Though some Mozart lovers will cite other Mozart works that they prefer, favorites that they listen to again and again, what no one questions is the power of this piece to probe the meaning of existence.

SO MANY RECORDINGS OF THE REQUIEM, in all of the different versions (another of which, by Richard Maunder, purports to eliminate Süssmayr's contributions), makes choosing a matter of education as well as taste. The more you listen, the more you may wish to compare, not only the interpretations of a host of conductors but the variety of musical texts on which the recordings are based. A reissued Sony release of Helmuth Rilling's recording of the Süssmayr-assisted score, with the Gachinger Kantorei and the Bach Collegium, both of Stuttgart, is notable in part for the glorious singing of the late soprano Arleen Auger. Other excellent choices include Leonard Bernstein's with the Bavarian Radio Chorus and Orchestra on Deutsche Grammophon, available as well on a thrilling DVD, and at least two recordings led by Herbert von Karajan, one analog and the other digital, the latter with the Vienna Philharmonic Orchestra and the former with the Berlin Philharmonic Orchestra. For alternative versions, often with period instruments, look for the recordings of such conductors as John Eliot Gardiner, Christopher Hogwood, and Roger Norrington.

Many recordings of the Requiem, which clocks in at around forty-five minutes in the Süssmayr version, come with a second piece, often the C Minor

Christopher Hogwood and his group with early instruments, July 21, 1985.

Mass; *Exsultate, jubilate;* or *Ave verum corpus.* A fine, inexpensive recording of the mass, coupled with the less frequently performed Kyrie in D Minor, K. 341, is led by Michael Halász with the Nicolaus Esterházy Sinfonia and the Hungarian Radio and Television Chorus.

Barbara Hendricks will break your heart with her singing of the Laudate Dominum in the Vespers, K. 339. The veteran Mozart maestro Sir Neville Marriner conducts the Academy of St. Martin in the Fields Chorus and Orchestra in this luminous 1985 EMI CD.

SELECTED OTHER CHORAL WORKS

Exsultate, jubilate, K. 165

A youthful work, thought by some to be Mozart's first real claim to greatness, *Exsultate, jubilate* in F major is an extended solo for Mozart's favorite vocal part, the soprano, with a small orchestra. Written in the form of a motet, the three-movement piece lasts about a quarter of an hour, but who's counting? Especially thrilling is the extended Alleluia, which is the entire "text" of the Allegro. Mozart puts the soprano through her paces, although the she was a he when Mozart wrote the piece for the Italian castrato Rauzzini.

Vespers, K. 339

Mozart composed two sets of vespers (music to be performed at an evening church service). For Mozart, these were among the occasional pieces of church music he composed, which include several litanies and a fairly large group of what were called epistle sonatas. The K. 339 Vespers, one of his last Salzburg compositions, stands out in large part because of the astoundingly beautiful soprano solo with chorus in the work's Laudate Dominum. This five and half minutes of music, which Mozart may have spent all of five and half minutes writing, are the kind of thing that used to discourage Mozart's contemporaries, particularly composers, who if they were honest with themselves had to admit that it was unlikely they would ever achieve such heights of stately, solemn, inspiring sublimity.

Ave verum corpus, K. 618

Ave verum corpus was one of the last pieces Mozart wrote, and for many listeners it is even more memorable than the fabled Requiem. Mozart made a gift of this short beauty to the organist Anton Stoll, who played and taught in Baden, where Mozart's wife, Constanze, was taking a cure at the spa. This motet is scored for chorus, strings, and organ. Nothing dramatic happens in it: the sun rises, the sun sets, the earth turns.

Masonic Cantata, K. 623

One of several so-called Masonic works Mozart wrote after becoming a Mason, this piece has the sad distinction of being the last that Mozart finished. The choral part here is all male, with memorable solos for tenor and, to a lesser extent, bass. Think of this as a musical bookend to some of the earliest compositions Mozart wrote, including his first cantata, K. 42, which came into the world in 1767, when Mozart was all of eleven years old.

This Mostly Mozart poster from 1974 came from a screen print by Jack Bush.

Requiem, K. 626

Maybe the most famous of all Mozart works, although certainly not necessarily the greatest—but why categorize?—this unfinished masterpiece long ago entered the pantheon of musical legend because Mozart was still working on it when he died. Entire books have been devoted simply to explicating which parts Mozart did indeed complete and which were the handiwork of his pupil Süssmayr; other musicians, including contemporary ones, have also attempted their own versions. So, best to put debate aside and simply surrender to this music's majesty, its power from the very first solemn chords to put us completely in its thrall. In the Mozart-Süssmayr version, there are eight sections: Introitus, Kyrie, Sequenz (consisting of Dies irae, Tuba mirum, Rex tremendae, Recordare, Confutatis, and Lacrimosa), Offerorium (consisting of Domine Jesu and Hostias), Sanctus, Benedictus, Agnus Dei, and Communio-Lux Aeterna. Especially well-known moments in this especially well-known piece are the thrilling chorus entry in the Dies irae, the trombone solo in the Tuba mirum, the extraordinary orchestral intervals that open and then continue under the chorus of the Rex tremendae, the exposed strings in the Recordare, the beautiful choral Sanctus, and the piercing Communio. Mozart, according to an account his sister-in-law wrote in a letter many years after Mozart's death, was possessed of this piece as he took his last breaths, mouthing the sound of the timpani. "I can still hear it now," she wrote.

MUSINGS ON

James Levine on Mozart's impact

Mozart means so very much to us; in his short life he gave us everything. To this day, I continue to study and perform as much Mozart as I can every year—opera, symphonic and choral works, chamber music, solo vocal works with orchestra or piano—and it's still not enough.

Mozart was able to encompass an emotional and psychological complexity in his music that remains unparalleled even today. He was so sympathetic and empathetic about human nature, about human foibles. This is particularly evident in his great operas, but one can hear it in the purely instrumental pieces as well. The sheer proliferation of ideas and the contrast, simplicity, and subtlety in his music are astonishing. There are already many glimpses of this in his early works (which can also be terrific in their own right). The more sophisticated, even subtler versions come later, in so many varied contexts and combinations, with differences of atmosphere, color, instrumentation, and mood that never fail to amaze, however familiar the music—as we know so well, for example, from the last three symphonies and countless other works. The achievement remains startling beyond comprehension.

It's generally agreed that the three Mozart–Da Ponte operas—*Figaro, Don Giovanni*, and *Così fan tutte*—are

among the perfect collaborations in opera between composer and librettist. But even before those, Mozart had
already proved himself a master of portraying human emotions and relationships on the stage, in his opera seria
Idomeneo and his comic masterpiece *Die Entführung aus
dem Serail*. And then two more operatic masterpieces—*Die
Zauberflöte* and *La clemenza di Tito*—followed the collaborations with Da Ponte!

What Mozart achieved seems even more remarkable
when one realizes that all of the works just mentioned were
accomplished in a single decade. *Idomeneo* was premiered
in 1781, *La clemenza di Tito* in 1791; he composed the three
last symphonies in 1788, in a single summer! Throughout
this time he was also producing a seemingly infinite variety
of other music, not to mention dealing with the vagaries and
difficulties of day-to-day life. He died two months short of his
thirty-sixth birthday. It's hard to imagine how much more we
might have had from him, and even harder to comprehend
how the course of music might have been changed, had he
not died so young.

James Levine is music director of both the Metropolitan
Opera and the Boston Symphony Orchestra.

Piano Music

"Like a cherub," Salieri says of Mozart in Pushkin's play *Mozart and Salieri*, "he brings to us some songs of paradise. And wakens in us children of the dust/A wingless longing—then he flies away!"

In reality, alas for Salieri and providentially for us, the very opposite is the case: what wakens or stirs within anyone lucky enough to hear Mozart remains, grows, develops. The more we hear of Mozart, the more the impact of his music multiplies our pleasure, our calm, grateful, thrilled sense that in spite of whatever may be wrong in the world, something good always remains, if not triumphs. In conception and execution, Mozart brings order to the chaos around us, nowhere more so than in the music he wrote for his most beloved instrument, the piano.

Accustomed as we are to think of Mozart first and foremost as a composer, we should remember that during his brief lifetime, his fame turned most importantly on his virtuosity as a pianist. During much of his career, he made a major portion of his living as a performer on the piano, playing either solo or chamber works that he had composed or appearing as soloist with an orchestra in one of his many splendid concertos. Within the orbit of what is now Austria and many of its Western European neighbors, Wolfgang Amadeus Mozart the pianist was a star, a box-office draw, a celebrity. If you were to speak of him in the patois of our current culture, he was "the man."

What a guy! Picture this: broke, worried about his wife's health, bothered by the latest entreaty from his caring but meddling father, Mozart again and again might have felt his life spinning out of control. Lesser mortals would retreat to bottle or betrayal (of self, of supporters); he, instead, turned to his art. Though we may see Mozart in our minds as some kind of supernatural savant, calling down ideas and inspiration from the heavens, he was very much a person of real flesh and blood, prone to anxiety, concerned about putting food on the table for his small family (only two of his children grew to adulthood, and one of them was not even born until the year of Mozart's death).

Unfortunately, an effete, porcelainlike image of Mozart still survives in the caricatures that introduce him in old textbooks and uninformed conversation. Though in physical presence he was short of stature and not especially handsome, with a face whose penetrating eyes were its dominant feature, Mozart was an imposing figure onstage once he took a seat at his piano and began to play. By all accounts, his technique was supple and adroit, his phrasing exquisite, the power of his fingers and arms explosive, and the feeling of his interpretation—odd word, since he was usually playing music he composed—deeply affecting. The echo of that greater performance, the whole of all those separate parts carries across the centuries.

Concertos and Sonatas

Strictly speaking, these two genres within Mozart's over-all catalog of music don't belong in the same category. But his achievement within each is strikingly similar in certain ways, and not simply because of the commonality of the instrument. As a composer of both concertos and sonatas, Mozart typically went at the job in prolonged bursts of energy and focus, so that his production of each divides itself fairly neatly into definable chronological periods. Moreover, his creativity in whatever he was doing was never selfish; he was not in the habit of hold-ing back in one area to save himself for something else. The well of his talent, in other words, seemed bottomless, and he composed accordingly, never so far as we know experiencing anything remotely resembling a composer's version of writer's block.

And when it came to the piano, Mozart clearly com-posed because it gave him such enormous pleasure. You can hear this emotion in every measure, even in the way one work seems to lead to another. In fact, Mozart rarely wrote only one of either; sonata upon sonata, concerto upon concerto was the usual pattern, set from the very beginning.

That beginning was earlier in the concerto form than in the sonata, and, if truth be told, the first few concertos are wonderful pieces but not the masterworks that would follow. Perhaps it is another way of indicating the com-poser's genius that we should even remark on this; little past the age of twenty-one Mozart was writing music for the piano as beautiful and, in its own concentrated way, as thrilling as anything that anyone else has composed since.

All told, he wrote twenty-seven or, some say, twenty-eight piano concertos and seventeen or eighteen piano sonatas, plus several pieces—rondos and fantasies—that more or less could stand as part of one or the other. In a career as short and productive as Mozart's, this was a singular achievement, but it's not really quantity here that astounds. For all intents and purposes, Mozart in these pieces invented piano music as we have known it ever since, an additionally amazing feat given the limitations of the actual instrument of his day. How did he do it?

There are many possible explanations, although none can fully explain the accomplishment. As with almost everything he wrote, with the very occasional exception of such pieces as the *Haydn* Quartets, Mozart worked at lightning speed. His twentieth piano concerto, K. 466, for example, was completed in early February 1785, and by almost exactly a month later he had knocked off the next one, K. 467, although he had been busy in the interim with other performances and a visit from his father. He was probably also helped in this regard by the fact that he could fill in some of his own part at the last

Mozart's Instrument

Not the least of the remarkable aspects of Mozart the pianist and Mozart the composer for piano is the fact that the instrument he played and for which he composed was quite unlike what we are familiar with today.

The most startling difference may have been the instrument's range: there were fewer notes, so the keyboard was shorter. His concert piano, which was made by a Viennese man named Anton Walter, has been preserved, and a few pianists have even recorded on it.

Another feature of Mozart's instrument, called a forte-piano, is that it lacked the pedals we are accustomed to seeing and using, or hearing used, today. During the last half-dozen years of his life, Mozart actually added a second instrument, a pedal piano to fit underneath the regular one. But the pedals on this second piano did not act as do those on modern pianos, which can control certain dynamics and tonal gradations of length. Mozart's pedal piano worked in the way that pedals work on an organ—an instrument, by the way, on which Mozart was also an expert and for which he even wrote some music.

Even with the limitations of his instrument, Mozart, was able to push the envelope past his contemporaries' achievements and create piano music that is still considered brilliant today on our less limited instruments.

minute, something he often did, since he was a world-class improviser.

Which leads to a second, more crucial explanation for Mozart's accomplishments for the piano: he could play. It seems elementary, but no composer, however talented, comes with a built-in knowledge of the instruments for which he is writing. Mozart's technical ability as a pianist astounded almost everyone who heard him; even the great Clementi, who wrote some of the first piano sonatas (still used as models by students today), was bested in an informal competition held soon after Mozart took up residence in Vienna.

Had Mozart been content simply to show off that talent, however, he need never have progressed much past his first concerto efforts, which began when he wrote his first four at only eleven years of age. But in listening to them and the four that followed, you can get the impression that something was nagging at him, a frustration with convention, a restlessness.

What to do?

It was a nice problem for someone so young and already so accomplished, who by the age of twenty (when he composed his sixth, seventh, and eighth piano concertos) was already welcome wherever in Western Europe music was held in high esteem. If Mozart was not a household name by then, he was rapidly becoming one. This was also not long after he had written his first few piano sonatas—five in 1774, when he was eighteen, and a sixth the following year. And, of course, he was writing lots of other music, too, something we must keep reminding ourselves of, in part because it is easy to forget or overlook, given what we might think of as normal human standards of creativity.

So, then, what happened? What jolt to a system or a psyche that was already seemingly supercharged?

It is one of the many tantalizing mysteries that Mozart's oeuvre keeps putting before us, no different really than our asking what drove him several years later to write his three last symphonies over the summer of 1788 or, a little earlier, to transport the art of opera someplace he—and it—had never before been. Whatever the explanation, it is clear in the music Mozart wrote for piano that some-time after his twenty-first birthday, he posed a problem to himself: *what can I do to change the very idea of a piano concerto?* The solution, as always, came in the notes.

Suddenly, with his ninth piano concerto, K. 271, Mozart had entered an entirely new territory for his instrument,

immensely more complicated on a technical level than anything that had preceded it and hugely, profoundly, astoundingly—what superlative can be sufficient?—*moving*. It is as
if in this concerto, with its dramatic first movement and
taut third bracketing an Andantino of piercing emotional
power, Mozart has at once stripped himself of all artifice
and disguise and offered an exuberance, a joie de vivre, that
is all the more contagious and pulsating because it comes
as well with a cry of anguish, deep calling unto deep.

What has happened here and will again with ever
greater frequency, not only in his writing for piano
but in just about everything he touched, is very personal. The ninth piano concerto for Mozart is a eureka
event, a watershed, not only in his career but truly in
the art of music. Previously, even in such musical monu-
ments as those that defined Bach's greatness, people
did not perceive music as an art of personal expression. But no one hearing Mozart play this concerto
could separate the music from the musician. The music
was the musician, or the musician was the music.
The composer of this piece was forevermore an artist.

We are accustomed now to think immediately in
such terms, to elevate all sorts of mediocrities into
something they are not, giving them a status they do
not deserve merely because the composer (or the writer
or the filmmaker or whoever) has ostensibly expressed
himself or herself. But in Mozart's case here, the fact of
such expression alone is shocking because it is so new.
And the impact is immediate and lasting because the art
of the expression is so intricate, clever, comprehensive,
and true. It is an art free of forced effects, in full command
of its material, confident, integrating form and function
in a sequence that is logical, interesting, and alive.

As if momentarily exhausted from the mental and psychological effort this breakthrough represented—not to mention the physical challenge as well of playing the piano at this level—Mozart took a little break, as it were, a kind of retrenchment while he was occupied with other challenges, musical and personal. And so it was not until 1784, at the ripe age of twenty-eight, by which time he had also taken several giant piano steps with his sonatas, that he wrote another piano concerto—no. 15, K. 450— of an emotional and technical magnitude of the ninth.

After which Mozart went on a run of piano concerto greatness that has no equal in the work of any other composer for both its quality and its quantity. In the space of just two years, he wrote ten more, and each one is a gem. All but two—no. 20 in D minor, K. 466, and no. 24 in C minor, K. 491—were in major keys. Each, written for a specific occasion, received its premiere with the composer at the piano. All were composed during what was arguably the period of Mozart's greatest popularity

Cadenzas

If the cadenzas in Mozart's concertos are less theatrical than those in, say, one of Rachmaninoff's four piano concertos, the reason lies less in the talent of the player than in the sensibility of the composer. It would have been totally out of keeping with the spirit and substance of his music had Mozart inserted into his concertos a moment in which the pianist basically showed up the rest of the musicians. Mozart the performer never needed to upstage the musicians with whom he was playing; looked at one way, the music took care of that. It always retained primary importance. This can seem a syllogism until we remember that, for Mozart, the aim of a concert was not to validate his ego, even if an enormous ego may have been the engine of his ambition.

That said, the cadenzas of Mozart's that have survived (K. 624) exhibit the usual traits of his music—the logic, the "rightness" of gesture, the absence of cheap tricks—just as they also signal that the man who wrote them could not only play but improvise. It is hard to imagine Mozart not adding an improvisatory flourish to one of his cadenzas. He was always tinkering with his scores when he had time, constantly making changes in his operas, for different example. The musical "text" was a living document.

and productivity. Every single one of them, today, appears on concert programs around the world.

Though not as showy as the big Romantic concertos that came from Beethoven, Brahms, Chopin, and others in the nineteenth century, they are technically demanding in ways that test the finest pianists. They require, first of all, a refinement of technique that cannot hide behind grand gesture. Mozart in these concertos and the two that followed afterward—the Coronation Concerto in 1788, K. 537, and the final twenty-seventh in B-flat major, K. 595, written during the last year of his life—challenge the pianist to exhibit what he or she can do without showing off. The music is thus expansive, even as the person playing it must be contained, a seeming paradox that Mozart would repeat, for example, in the arias of his great operas.

Meanwhile, Mozart was also writing ever more beautiful sonatas—and, to repeat, all this time, chamber music, opera, symphonies, and even piano music other than concertos and sonatas. He was now married. He had established himself as the preeminent pianist of his time in Vienna, if not elsewhere. He continued to tour, though not with the frequency of his childhood. And he was not yet thirty years old.

What a rush this must have been, something even Mozart more or less admitted in the tone, if not the contents, of his letters to Leopold. Many of the missives from this period run to several pages each, as if no detail of his life were not worth sharing. Yet the ardor with which he went about reporting each event—a performance somewhere, problems with a copyist, difficulty with a loan repayment, a singer's foibles—seems to represent a deeper engagement with life itself, with the fact of life, not only its mystery or frequent pain or inevitable sadness but its glory, the incredible, amazing, indefinable reality of being alive in the world.

Looking back and knowing what we do about how Mozart's life ended, it is perhaps inevitable that we see his achievement through the prism of his passing—a word he would have hated. But the remarkable aspect of his day-to-day life as recounted in the documents that have been left to us (mostly, the family correspondence) is that Mozart was too busy, too productive, to be thinking daily about his own death. What we hear, instead, is a deep, abiding passion for every minute of every day, framed or formed by an intelligence that is always intimate with our common mortality. "Rejoice," is Mozart's message in a word of our own invention. "Lament not."

As if to celebrate his good fortune, Mozart wrote all of these sonatas and concertos for piano. As if to remind us to count our blessings, he kept returning to this favored instrument. As if to challenge himself, he kept finding new ways to explore the human condition with the explication of notes in an infinity of combinations played out on a neat, orderly arrangement of black and white keys.

Order. A word that always accompanies Mozart's accomplishment in his piano composition. Order begets form, and form begets beauty; form in Mozart's piano concertos and sonatas *is* beauty.

If we listen just two or three times to virtually any movement of any of these beautiful pieces, we find ourselves unable to get the music out of our heads. Lucky us. We listen, for example, soon after the opening of Concerto no. 25, K. 503, to the upward scales and the downward arpeggios, the orchestra daring the piano to stay with its declaration, and we suddenly realize that we, too, are along for the ride. We have company. The music goes with us, it travels wherever we wander, a new constant in our lives, a sonic beacon, if you will.

This miraculous piece, which Mozart wrote in 1786 at the age of thirty, bears comparison to a much longer work in a different genre that Mozart also finished that same year, his opera *The Marriage of Figaro.* What strikes us about both is the relatively simple means with which Mozart's art becomes so dramatic. It is never in Mozart the isolated fragment or the individual element of a chord, a key, some counterpoint that gives the music its buoyancy. Rather, the way in which Mozart employed the tools he had at hand accounts for the effect his music almost always achieves, in the case of the twenty-fifth piano concerto an overwhelming sense of urgency.

As the piano responds to the orchestra's pliant call, we feel without knowing any of the inner details the drama of Mozart's own life, his triumphant struggle to overcome the odds of ignorant patronage, disloyal friends, or recalcitrant colleagues. None of this comes out as a whine; the music could not be less self-pitying.

Nor, on the other hand, is it sentimentally optimistic or indulgently platitudinous. Listen, now, to one of the late sonatas, the Sonata in C Major, K. 545, from that momentous year for Mozart of 1788. This well-known piece, which Mozart wrote either for a beginning student or because he hoped it would appeal to the market of such beginners (and therefore bring him some much-needed income), makes no claim on the greater issues of the day. It is neither a sop nor a plea; it simply *is*, and if anyone else were to take its ingredients and remix them, chances are excellent that the result would be porous. But here, as elsewhere in Mozart, it holds.

SURELY IN NO OTHER GENRE WITHIN Mozart's oeuvre, except perhaps for opera, is the variety and breadth of both live and recorded performance as great as it is in his piano concertos and sonatas. There are so many different ways of coming at this music that to hear it as performed by many different artists is to understand it—not completely, never completely, but certainly in greater and ever grander

Now retired, Alicia de Larrocha appeared
numerous times at the Mostly Mozart Festival.
Here, she rehearses for Great Performers at
Lincoln Center, April 27, 1975.

increments. Bringing her or his talent and sensibility
to the performance, each artist reveals a version of the
basic human truth that lies at the heart of this music.
It is as if the more the music is divided among a larger
number of performers, the more its magnificence, its
range and reach, multiplies.

Among contemporary pianists, an initial divide
separates those who play Mozart from those who,
for temperamental or other reasons, do not. Then,
among those who play or at least have tried to play
Mozart, one group includes pianists who have made
an occasional Mozart recording and another consists

Daniel Barenboim, October 3, 1990.

of those who have plunged into the entire repertoire, or at least a good portion of it. Several extraordinary musicians fall into this latter category, among them Daniel Barenboim, Alfred Brendel, Alicia de Larrocha, Murray Perahia, Andras Schiff, and Mitsuko Uchida, while in the former such standouts as Richard Goode loom large in quality, even if not yet in quantity (he is working his way through all of the concertos).

Ideally, the way to jump into this exhilarating music is to listen to as many of the concertos as possible, one after the other, with a sonata or two mixed in, and not worry for now about which number is which. Nor is it helpful at first to pay particular attention to the artist. Play what you can find and immerse yourself in it, in the music. Mozart would have subscribed to this approach. He would not have expected the casual listener to decon-struct how each movement of each piece is organized.

"The most important thing in music is not to be found in the notes," Gustav Mahler said, a century after Mozart's reign as composer nonpareil and at the height of his own fame in the same cultural capital of Vienna. Mozart would have understood what Mahler meant by this paradoxical statement, for, of course, without the notes there is no music (unless your name is John Cage and you are composing one of your famous silences). But the notes themselves do not make *music*. Mozart, this most highly trained of musicians, who made arguably the most successful transition in music history from prodigy to master, knew his stuff. But he would have been happy simply to hear your applause, eager to solicit your patronage, and understanding of the probable level of your musical education.

Though he suffered no fools, Mozart was touchingly sympathetic to the whys and wherefores of life, to the foibles and follies of his fellow man. Especially in his operas, his humanity is gracefully yet forcefully evident. But that same characteristic is strongly apparent in his piano concertos and sonatas, because he wrote them to be heard. He wanted people to enjoy the experience of hearing him play these intoxicating pieces. He had a keen sense, developed in part through his contact with men and women from all walks of life, about what worked and didn't work from a dramatic standpoint. He wanted his music to give pleasure, and he not only knew how to achieve this but also kept thinking of new ways to do so. You needn't be a musicologist to get it.

But just as someone entering, say, the Sistine Chapel immediately marvels at the sense of proportion revealed in Michelangelo's masterpiece whether or not he or she possesses formal artistic background or training, so the man or the woman hearing Mozart's piano concertos will be instantly and thoroughly overcome by the same sense of dumbstruck awe. The logic of the music, the coherence and brilliance of its design, stands out unobtrusively but incontrovertibly. You needn't have seen the movie classic *Elvira Madigan* to grasp the formal beauty of its sound track, the Andante of Mozart's Piano Concerto no. 21 in C Major, K. 467 (recorded by, among many others, pianist Malcolm Bilson in an especially moving Archiv disc under John Eliot Gardiner leading the English Baroque Soloists on authentic period instruments).

The nineteenth-century composer Hector Berlioz once jokingly wrote in a letter to a friend, later published in his great *Memoirs*, "If you were to go to the piano and play something from your favourite composers . . . I should probably interrupt you in a pet, saying that it was really time to have done with this admiration for Mozart, whose operas are all exactly alike, and whose *sang-froid* provokes and wearies me."

Joking aside, one could actually take Berlioz's contention seriously with regard to Mozart's writing for the piano—but with the caveat that to say they are "exactly alike" would be to compliment them for the similarity of their intelligence, beauty, and construction. Consider, for example, the wonderfully assertive opening of the first movement of Mozart's Piano Concerto no. 23, K. 488, wherein he gives the strings and then the full orchestra first crack at the first melody, which becomes ambiguous in its emotional thrust. One thinks suddenly of the way in which the clarinets were given prominence at the beginning of the previously composed concerto, no. 22, K. 482. The more things change, the more they sound . . . well, not alike, but of a kind . . . sui generis.

As you listen more often to these concertos, the dawning truth of their simultaneous sameness and uniqueness becomes obvious, especially when you go back and begin to compare the interpretations of different soloists. And so, for example, the muscularity of that opening sequence of scales and arpeggios in Concerto no. 25 jumps out at you with the performance of Alfred Brendel (in a terrific live Philips recording, made in 1978, under the baton of Sir Neville Marriner with the Academy of St. Martin in the Fields). But go from there to the same moment in the same piece in the recording of Mitsuko Uchida, part of her complete Mozart concerto series with Jeffrey Tate and the English Chamber Orchestra, also on Philips, and you sense something else, the fluidity of the phrasing, the felicitousness of the interplay between orchestra and piano when the latter eventually picks up the same motif.

Now, let us turn the tables and play as much of this music as we can but always by the same performer. Again, there are so many superb pianists to choose from, but it would be difficult to make a better choice than that of Murray Perahia, whose complete recording of the concertos as pianist and conductor with the English Chamber Orchestra is a landmark in both Mozart's music and recorded piano music.

These recordings from the 1980s, the first for the American-born Perahia, later reissued by Sony Classical, illuminate our understanding not only of the music but also of the art of playing the piano. Perahia, who after some health issues that included a thumb injury in the early 1990s, has subsequently recorded works by Bach, Chopin, and Schubert, among others. Nuance of touch, dexterity of finger-ing, command of tone color and volume, and feeling for the emotional range of the music define Perahia's approach to Mozart—if *approach* is even the proper word. *Reverence* might be better, though not in a reli-gious sense and certainly not with any intimation of preciousness. These are performances in which the full measure of Mozart's art astounds and inspires.

"We drove to [your brother's] first subscription con-cert, at which a great many members of the aristocracy were present," Leopold Mozart reported to his daughter, Nannerl, in a letter from Vienna dated February 16, 1785. "The concert was magnificent and the orchestra played splendidly," Papa Mozart continued proudly, mentioning each work in sequence. "Then we had a new and very fine concerto [no. 20, K. 466] by Wolfgang, which the copyist was still copying when we arrived, and the rondo of which your brother did not even have time to play through, as he had to supervise the copying."

A year afterward, the same concerto in D minor, no. 20, comes up again in a letter to Nannerl from her father, who is this time back in Salzburg, where he is writing about a performance of the work by a differ-ent pianist. "Marchand . . . played it from the score and [Michael] Haydn turned over the pages for him and at the same time had the pleasure of seeing with what art it is composed, how delightfully the parts are interwoven and what a difficult concerto it is. I chose this one, since you have the clavier parts of all the others and I still possessed the score of this one. We rehearsed it in the morning," he adds, by which piece of information we may conclude that Leopold was the conductor.

By then, Mozart fils had embarked on a new phase of his career, the composition and, in 1786, the premiere of his first operatic masterpiece, *The Marriage of Figaro.* With the success of that work, followed soon by the commission for another (*Don Giovanni*), Mozart's period of intense piano creativity would come to a close. He would write only two more concertos after 1786, and there would be an attendant decline in his public performances as a pianist. Soon, Mozart's genius as a pianist would enter the realm of the legends that came to surround him. No doubt, like the stories that make the rounds today of the celebrated and talented, any number of noblemen and common folk would insist they had heard the great man in live performance. By the time the last person who could honestly make that claim had died, the concerto as a form had been hugely augmented and ornamented by composers who were not yet born

Brendel Speaks

"One characteristic of Mozart's music is the contrast between the public and the private," said Alfred Brendel in an interview in the *New York Review of Books.* "Further contrasts in Mozart include: the fateful and the personal; the galant and graceful, and the sublime; the comic and the serious; the ironic and the unequivocal."

Brendel, whose reissued Mozart concerto recordings from the 1970s are treasures, retired in 2008 as a performing concert pianist. Born in Czechoslovakia in 1931 to Austrian parents, he shares with Mozart the distinction of having basically taught himself to play. The author of several books, Brendel is a fine writer whose intelligence can seem a little daunting. It is a quality that drives his playing, not only of Mozart's piano concertos; listen, for example, to his live recording of the eighth and ninth piano sonatas, K. 310 and 311, and you may almost feel part of the compositional process, as if with Mozart you were working things out. And then, how the piano sings!

"Mozart is one of the most sensuous composers ever. There is a sensuality too about his melodies. . . . Busoni said there was no doubt Mozart took singing as his starting point, and from this stems the uninterrupted melodiousness which shimmers through his compositions."

when Mozart himself died. But the royal line, the musical succession, would always trace back to Amadeus.

Other Works with Piano

In addition to his writing for solo piano, Mozart also composed a great deal of other music for his own instrument. He wrote several sonatas for two pianos at a time when this was almost unheard of. He also composed a concerto for two pianos, K. 365 (which is available today in a splendid Sony Classical CD with Murray Perahia and Radu Lupu). His chamber works include two fabulous piano quartets, six piano trios, and a piano and wind quintet, all of which have also been recorded by a variety of musicians. Mozart, in fact, may be the most recorded classical musician in history, although it would be a challenge to compute and then compare, given not only the backlog of reissues but the enormous number of budget labels that continue to spring up, even as the industry itself goes through a reinvention because of the Internet.

Not every great pianist was smitten with Mozart. The late iconoclast Glenn Gould disparaged him, but Gould's opinion is an egregious exception. Mozart himself, in a rare boast to his father when he was twenty-two years old, writing about "a man of superior talent," added that "without being Godless, I cannot deny [this] is true in my own case."

SELECTED PIANO CONCERTOS

Accustomed as we are in today's computer era to the illusion of the neat, orderly tracking of virtually anything, it can come as a disturbing revelation that the music of one as eminent as Mozart should present a messy or even mysterious challenge to the cataloger. Although Mozart kept a log of his compositions during much of his adult life, many of his piano concertos were written when he was young. In addition, one of them, no. 10, K. 365, is for two pianos, and another, earlier one, no. 7, K. 242, is for three pianos. An even earlier work, no. 5, K. 107, is actually an arrangement by Mozart of three piano sonatas by J. S. Bach, and the previous concertos one through four are also arrangements of music by other people.

Nevertheless, these pieces are all counted in the typical total of twenty-seven—which, however, excludes two concert rondos, one of which is only a single movement. Thus, the evident confusion about how many piano concertos Mozart actually wrote, or, more precisely, how many of his works for piano and orchestra should be classified as concertos. A similar debate can grow out of an examination of his symphonic output, usually capped at forty-one (with the caveat that he did not write most of the thirty-seventh), but potentially confusing if you attempt to account for numerous symphonic fragments and references to works or partial works that are completely missing.

All of this attests as well to the phenomenal pace at which Mozart produced music of all kinds and to the reality that most of his music was written for a single reason—to be performed. He was, in other words, usually preoccupied with the task at hand or simply too busy to be bothered by precise questions of dating, numerating, and/or categorizing. We should worry less and enjoy more.

SELECTED PIANO CONCERTOS

Concerto no. 9 in E-flat Major, K. 271

The ninth concerto is the piece in which Mozart, at the age of twenty-one, found his groove both as a composer of concertos for the piano and as a composer, period. The innovations begin at the very beginning, when Mozart has the piano come in right away. But it's what the piano does expressively that makes this music so extraordinary. This is especially apparent in

MUSINGS ON

Alfred Brendel with advice on playing Mozart

Let this be the first warning to the Mozart performer: piano playing, be it ever so faultless, must not be considered sufficient. Mozart's piano works should be for the player a receptacle full of latent musical possibilities which often go far beyond the purely pianistic. It is not the limitations of Mozart's pianoforte (which I refuse to accept) that point the way, but rather Mozart's dynamism, colourfulness and expressiveness in operatic singing, in the orchestra, in ensembles of all kinds. For example, the first movement of Mozart's Sonata in A minor K. 310 is to me a piece for symphony orchestra; the second movement resembles a vocal scene with a dramatic middle section, and the finale could be transcribed into a wind divertimento with no trouble at all.

In Mozart's piano concertos, the sound of the piano is set off more sharply against that of the orchestra. Here the human voice and the orchestral solo instrument will be the main setters of standards for the pianist. From the Mozart singer he will learn not only to sing but also to 'speak' clearly and with meaning, to characterize, to act and react; from the string player to think in terms of up-bow and down-bow; and from the flautist or oboist

the second-movement Andantino, a stately, lyrical soaring in which the piano seems not so much to be played as to sing. The highly energetic third-movement Rondo (Presto) brings this piece to a highly charged close.

to shape fast passages in a variety of articulations, instead of delivering them up to an automatic non-legato or, worse still, to an undeviating legato such as the old complete edition prescribed time and again without a shred of authenticity.

A singing line and sensuous beauty, important as they may be in Mozart, are not, however, the sole sources of bliss. To tie Mozart to a few traits is to diminish him. That great composers have manifold things to say and can use contradictions to their advantage should be evidence in performances of his music. There has been altogether too much readiness to reduce Mozart to Schumann's 'floating Greek gracefulness' or Wagner's 'genius of light and love'. Finding a balance between freshness and urbanity ('He did not remain simple and did not grow over-refined,' said Busoni), force and transparency, unaffectedness and irony, aloofness and intimacy, between freedom and set patterns, passion and grace, abandonment and style—among the labours of the Mozart player, this is only rewarded by a stroke of good luck.

From *Music Sounded Out: Essays, Lectures, Interviews, Afterthoughts* (1990)

Concerto no. 15 in B-flat Major, K. 450

The fifteenth concerto is a terrific piece that begins quietly and builds incrementally into a dazzling display of piano-orchestra coordination, some bravura technique, and an unerring sense of pace and feel.

MUSINGS ON

Emmanuel Ax on Mozart's piano concertos

One of the great privileges of being a piano player is having the chance to study and perform Mozart's piano concertos. I know, there is an incredible amount of wonderfully exciting, profound, and meaningful music for our instrument; but surely pride of place must be given to these musical marvels. What makes them so special to us? I am sure that there are as many answers to that question as there are pianists—each person has a different response. But the enthusiasm, I believe, is universal.

For me, the special quality of the concertos is that I get to participate in a real opera without having a decent singing voice. Mozart was truly a man of the theater, and the great operas that he left—*Figaro, Don Giovanni, The Magic Flute*— have no equal in their combination of musical perfection and understanding of humanity. It is that special combination of musical and psychological excitement that is just as present in the piano concertos. When I am involved in a performance of the D minor Concerto, for instance, I can easily imagine being on the stage as some sort of Byronic hero, possibly even

The second-movement Andante, though short, is touching, and the concluding third-movement Allegro will lift you out of your seat with its taut yet graceful forward momentum.

Concerto no. 20 in D Minor, K. 466

One of only two Mozart piano concertos in a minor key, the twentieth concerto is also the seventh overall

a rake like Don Giovanni—for someone of my girth and weight, a very special attraction! But every concerto that he left us is like a miniature opera, and we even get to imagine our own characters and stories. The orchestral introductions are always full of anticipation, and the entrance of the soloist is almost always a moment of astonishment—a real coup de théâtre. Since Mozart, and largely through his example, the piano concerto became the great virtuoso vehicle for pianists—but no one did it better; in fact, only very few did it as well.

Playing these pieces is both frightening and exhilarating—frightening because most of the time you won't get it right, and exhilarating because you just might make a couple of phrases sound the way you imagined they should. There is a comfort, though—this music is so touching and exciting that you can't really ruin all of it, even if you get it all wrong in performance. I hope to keep trying to do it right for a few years to come, and I think we are all lucky to have the Mostly Mozart Festival, where we get to hear these amazing pieces and share some of Mozart's genius, at least for an evening.

in a remarkable run of twelve concertos that Mozart wrote in the years 1784 to 1786, beginning with the fourteenth, K. 449, and ending with the twenty-fifth, K. 503. The twentieth begins with a stirring rhythmic figure that the orchestra and the piano trade back and forth before the piano introduces a first theme, which the orchestra follows—the ideas come quickly and unceasingly in this unusually long opening movement.

The shorter, second-movement Romance might be the backdrop to a quiet, passionate courtship outside one of the palaces where Mozart often performed. The third-movement Allegro assai gets right to it, daring us to keep up with its fast-paced delicacy.

Concerto no. 21 in C Major, K. 467

Completed just a month after the twentieth concerto, the twenty-first, like its immediate predecessor, opens

---

MUSINGS ON *Mozart*

Dietrich Fischer-Dieskau on the D Minor Concerto

It was while I was at the conservatory—that is, during the war—that the pianist Wilhelm Kempff introduced me to three of Mozart's piano concertos. He played them in the Beethoven-Saal with a chamber orchestra conducted by Fritz Stein, who at the time was head of my music school. There is no way to describe the emotion that overcomes me when I first hear an important work by Mozart. I was sitting on the stage behind the orchestra; a sense of ecstasy filled me as these treasures reached my ear for the first time. I was especially fascinated with the soulful and at the same time unearthly way Kempff rendered the D-minor Concerto, both dramatic and precise. In some indeterminate way his conducting matched his appearance: blond hair, looking wind-blown, above a strong nose, a tall, slender body. . . . That evening I came close to taking him for a heavenly messenger.

From *Reverberations: The Memoirs of Dietrich Fischer-Dieskau* (1989)

---

with a very long first-movement Allegro maestoso. The second-movement Andante, half as long, made a splash as a movie sound track more than thirty years ago in *Elvira Madigan*, but that should not spoil our enjoyment of it as a superb example of the greatness of simplicity. The third-movement Allegro vivace assai is vivace indeed—short, fast, bursting with brio, and with a melody you will be humming to yourself afterward.

Concerto no. 22 in E-flat Major, K. 482

Another concerto with an extended first movement, the twenty-second was composed right around the time Mozart embarked on his first operatic collaboration with da Ponte, *The Marriage of Figaro*. Whether by chance or by design, the concerto bears a sonic resemblance to the tonal brilliance of that opera's arias. Once again, a long first movement yields this time to both an extended Andante and a finale, marked Allegro-andante cantabile-tempo I, is nearly as long as the first. But length is hardly the point here. This is music you could play at either a wedding or a funeral, such is the complexity of emotions. The Andante, with its several nearly chromatic piano sequences broken by the most piercing of intervals, might be the piece you take with you to the proverbial desert isle.

Concerto no. 23 in A Major, K. 488

How many ways are there to shout "Bravo!"? Here in the twenty-third concerto, Mozart begins with a theme that is at once poignant and thrilling, the kind of music that, the moment you hear it, immediately changes your outlook on whatever else is going on in your life. Again, this is one of the concertos he wrote in the middle of *Figaro*, with a deeply moving second movement that seems to demand the burst of the Allegro that follows—the piano and the strings together in a moment that encapsulates the ability of these concertos to make and circumscribe a world.

Concerto no. 24 in C Minor, K. 491

Composed shortly after the twenty-third concerto, the twenty-fourth, the second of only two Mozart piano concertos in a minor key, begins disturbingly with a series of chords that takes us immediately into a kind of dark region—only to be followed in the second movement by a kind of contemplative mood, as if we need some space to be ready for the variations that play on the third movement's theme, minor to the very end.

Concerto no. 25 in C Major, K. 503

The twenty-fifth concerto may be the one Mozart piano concerto to own if you must choose only one. This stirring, gorgeous piece opens with an urgency in both piano and orchestra that never really lets up. This remarkable concerto, the last in the series of twelve that Mozart composed between 1784 and 1786, invites comparison with what Beethoven would do afterward with the form. An elegiac second-movement Andante is followed by an altogether brilliant Allegretto, and the entire concerto carries the weight and substance of a major symphony.

Concerto no. 26 in D Major, K. 537

One of the eloquences that emerged from the mysterious year of 1788, when Mozart composed his last three symphonies, the twenty-sixth concerto, which returns to the form of the piano concerto, is marked by an especially expressive second-movement Adagio, surely one of the most beautiful Mozart ever wrote and notable as well for its spare orchestration. Not performed until 1789—something of a mystery, since Mozart rarely wrote without an audience in mind—the piece is known as the Coronation Concerto because Mozart played it in 1790 at the coronation of Leopold II in Frankfurt am Main.

Concerto no. 27 in B-flat Major, K. 595

The twenty-seventh was Mozart's last piano concerto, composed during the last calendar year of his life but actually completed in early January 1791. Perhaps because he knew he would be playing its first performance, which he did in March 1791, there are places in the piece wherein the piano part shows only the first and last notes of a phrase. This presents an interesting challenge to performers, some of whom play only what Mozart notated, while others do what Mozart would have done, which is to fill in the blanks. The third-movement Allegro is notably joyful, an especially tender farewell to the form.

SELECTED PIANO SONATAS

Mozart's piano sonatas—like so many of his piano concertos, written in groups—are a world unto themselves,

A 1789 drawing made of Mozart from life is thought to
be the last portrait of the composer. (Unsigned drawing)

although, of course, they share obvious traits with the
larger works for piano and orchestra, their concerto cous-
ins. Throughout, Mozart's sonata writing is logical, highly
coherent, yet full of surprise and endowed with melodic
and harmonic beauty. Most of these pieces were written
because Mozart needed music of his own to play at the
frequent subscription concerts he presented or the recitals
he gave during his regular visits with friends among the
nobility. A few of the sonatas were composed for students,
notably one of the last, the Sonata in C Major, K. 545,
which Mozart indicated was for beginners. But you will

want to hear it played by someone who is not a beginner, and you will be astonished that a thing of such beauty could have been created from such modest intentions.

Late within the long span of his piano sonatas, Mozart wrote what he called a Fantasia in C Minor, K. 475, again for piano, and his final Sonata in F Major is built from two movements classified as K. 533 and an earlier Rondo, K. 494. The resulting bit of confusion sometimes leads to gentle debate over whether the total output of piano sonatas is eighteen or nineteen.

No matter. Enjoy them for what they are, music that broke the convention of the sonata as mere entertainment. And if you must choose, begin with the Sonata in A Major, K. 331, which opens with a lyrical Andante grazioso that is every bit as spare and yet developed as anything anyone has done since. The brief (little more than three-minute-long) closing Alla turca: Allegretto sounds especially thrilling on an original instrument.

SELECTED OTHER WORKS FOR PIANO

Depending on how you count, in addition to his piano concertos and sonatas Mozart wrote more than six dozen other works for solo piano—perhaps even more than that, because it is likely that any number of short works, composed more or less on the spur of the moment, have been lost.

Mozart's piano output here includes variations, minuets, preludes, fantasias, and dances. He also wrote several pieces for piano duet (two pianists, one piano), many of which would have been for him to perform with his sister, Nannerl, when they were touring as children.

A thrilling late variation of the form are two pieces written for two pianos, the Fugue in C Minor, K. 426, and the Sonata in D Major, K. 448.

Everything the mature Mozart composed for the piano grew out of his own experience as the most famous pianist of his day. In a way that we think of certain masters of painting as creators of work that is termed *painterly*, Mozart's piano writing sits naturally in the hand, never feels forced, always exhibits a kind of oneness with the instrument that paradoxically takes our immediate focus away from the piano and the pianist and places it instead where it should be, and always is in Mozart—on the *music*.

Listen to one of the great rondos he wrote in the middle of his production of piano concertos—the three-movement Rondo in D, K. 382, for example—and try if you can to keep from smiling and saying to yourself, "He did it again!" And what did he do? A marchlike beginning, a seductive, short Adagio fooling with the same theme, and then an even shorter Allegro, again repeating the basics of what we heard at the start. *What we hear*: not what we "think," not what we "notice," not what we "imagine," and certainly not what we "endure." Like the first flowering of a friendship, this music is borne aloft by the magnificence of its being.

Opera

If Mozart had written only four or five of his finest operas, we would still be talking about him. So great is his achievement in this genre that to analyze or criticize it is a little like having a review and a discussion of Shakespeare's *Hamlet, King Lear, Romeo and Juliet,* and *Macbeth.* On the one hand, what's to say? On the other . . . a lot.

Where to begin?

At the beginning. Mozart finished the first of his twenty-plus operas (do you count only completed works? only strict operas?) when he was eleven years old. He finished the last two shortly before he died, and one of them—*The Magic Flute*—is not only one of the greatest operas by anyone but arguably one of the most important and beautiful pieces of music ever written.

Of course, as we know, Mozart hardly confined himself to opera. But the fact that unlike Puccini, for example, Mozart wrote lots of other music only serves to delineate and heighten both the intrinsic excellence and the extrinsic interest of the operatic portion of his oeuvre.

Retrospectively, it may seem inevitable that Mozart would compose operas. For one thing, Mozart traveled frequently as a boy, and many of those trips took him to

Italy, opera's first home. No doubt, the family's touring there and elsewhere had something to do not only with exposing him to opera but also with planting in his head the idea that he could compose them, too.

"To tell the truth, it was the emperor himself who first gave me the idea of getting Wolfgangerl [a diminutive] to write an opera," Leopold reported from Vienna to his friend back in Salzburg. This was at the end of January 1768, so "Wolfgangerl" had just celebrated his twelfth birthday. The opera in question was something called *La finta semplice* (The Pretended Simpleton), which the young composer would indeed complete that year, along with another, shorter operatic work that he called *Bastien und Bastienne*. The boy wonder was on his way.

What a childhood! It has been the purview of any number of armchair psychologists and curious writers to make conjectures about the dynamics of the relationship between Mozart père and Mozart fils. A veritable school of analytical thought has focused especially on the evolution of what is arguably Mozart's finest operatic invention, *Don Giovanni*, which was completed after Leopold's death. Was the story of this opera a thematic representation of how Mozart felt about his father, the opera therefore his revenge for an unhappy upbringing?

Who can say? But on the evidence that was left to us, Mozart wasn't unhappy. Hard as it may be to comprehend, Mozart seems to have enjoyed his life as a wunderkind. Even the long, dreary days getting from one place to another, often staying in rooms so small he had to share a bed with his father, after an unappealing meal that the innkeeper scrounged up from leftovers, seem not to have discouraged the future progenitor of opera as we still know and love it.

MUSINGS ON

Renata Scotto on Italians singing Mozart

It's a funny thing about Mozart and Italian singers. Few Italian artists are given the chance to sing Mozart's Italian master-pieces, *Don Giovanni, Così fan tutte, Le nozze di Figaro.* Some time ago there was good reason to keep the Italians away, I admit. In our century, perhaps until the 1940s Mozart, along with Bellini and Verdi, was often sung with vulgar verismo exaggerations. *Norma* sounded like *Cavalleria,* and so did *Don Giovanni.* So at some point the Germans said, "Enough!" and took over, creating what many people now call the German Mozart Style. But Mozart *a la tedesca* is as wrong as the ver-ismo approach, because music is simply music. And often the singers who make a specialty of Mozart are so worried about creating *Kunst* that they forget to make theater. There is really no mystique or special difficulty about singing Mozart, and its importance is exaggerated by the keepers of the flame. We would be fortunate indeed if the same attention were always paid to the proper way to sing Bellini, Rossini, and Donizetti. When Mozart wrote Italian operas, despite what the Germans may say, he wrote Italian operas.

From *Scotto: More than a Diva* (1984)

How tempting the desire to imagine the thoughts and feelings of Mozart as he made his first youthful forays into this immensely fruitful area of his art. What we have to go on is the music, but that is more than evidence enough. Somehow, during all of those travels and their accompanying travails, Mozart was clearly becoming not

Fernando Botero's creation for the Mostly Mozart
festivities in 1984.

only the musician who would change the world but a
keen observer of his fellow man (and woman). The proof
is everywhere in the music, especially in the operatic
music. Mozart's operas overflow with characters whose
fears and longings, joys and tragedies, hopes, ambitions,
dreams, and desires are *ours*. Nor is this extraordinary

perception of—*into*—people something as simple as a case of archetypes made manifest.

The truly thrilling thing about the characters in Mozart's mature operas is the emotional range, depth, and verisimilitude of the music. We know Susanna's heartbreak in *The Marriage of Figaro* because Mozart literally put it into, what she sings. We recognize the consequences of Don Giovanni's fatal, final decision because we can hear it in the ominous chords that open and close the opera. When Fiordiligi and Dorabella are joined by Don Alfonso in the first act of *Così fan tutte* (Women Are Like That) to sing "Soave sia il vento" (May breezes blow lightly) as they bid what turns out to be a false farewell to Guglielmo and Ferrando, we are stirred not by the farcical story but by the exposed, lyrical beauty of the soaring song.

Technique alone, even on a level as stupendously high as that which Mozart's eventually reached, cannot accomplish this. Certainly, the composer of an enchantment on the dizzying aesthetic height of *The Magic Flute* had to know the human voice, the full palette of the orchestra, the fundamentals of harmony and counterpoint, and the demands of dramatic storytelling, including scenery, costumes, and even makeup. But something else had to happen repeatedly within Mozart as he composed this masterpiece, a courageous journey within himself, wherein he faced the perils and imponderables of the human heart unflinchingly and with complete honesty. To create musical life of this depth and caliber, Mozart had to know life himself, had to have experienced it, watched it, thought about it, and, ultimately and in every way possible, *felt* it. *This* was his great gift, which will continue giving as long as the music is heard.

MUSINGS ON

Placido Domingo on singing Mozart

Unless you are a born Mozart tenor, Mozart is the most difficult of all composers to sing. Young singers at the onset of their careers can probably get through Puccini and some other verismo composers without a good technique, at least for a while. But they couldn't get through Mozart (or Verdi) because in Mozart you are totally exposed. You have nothing to hide behind, you are vocally naked! Your ignorance would show up at once . . . And it's not true that Mozart cannot harm young voices. On the contrary: if you sing Mozart without a good technique you would soon strangle yourself. The repetitions of certain phrases are written in such a way that they could easily tire your throat. If you sang *"Un aura amorosa"* without a good technique, for instance, you would become unstuck after four bars!

From *Placido Domingo: My Operatic Roles*
by Helena Matheopoulos, 2003

Early Operas

Like a fabled poet writing long adolescent epics that give hints of what's to come, Mozart in his early opera efforts was already composing music that in fits and starts more than hinted at the towering achievements that would follow. Often these first productions were marred by a weak libretto, in other cases by the task of sustaining a still restrained musical vocabulary over the extended musical arc of a whole opera.

After a last such short effort, *Il re pastore* (The Shepherd King), K. 208, in 1775, when he was nineteen, Mozart was otherwise occupied until he turned twenty-three and seemingly out of nowhere composed what might have been his first true operatic success, *Zaide*, K. 344—if only he had finished it. Enough was completed that it has even been recorded (with German conductor Nikolaus Harnoncourt), but its missing libretto has made a real reconstruction impossible. Highlights include a lovely lullaby sung by the soprano who plays Zaide.

By the time Mozart abandoned this project, which for unknown reasons he was writing without a commission, he was looking for a way out of Salzburg. *Idomeneo*, which he composed the following year, in 1780, would become his farewell, and the opera that followed soon after, *Die Entführung aus dem Serail* (The Abduction from the Seraglio), his welcome to Vienna.

Operatic Terms

Much of the operatic tradition in Mozart's time had its origins in Italy, where two general forms of opera served as models for him as well. *Opera seria* and *opera buffa* are more or less self-explanatory, the former meaning "serious opera" and the latter "comic opera." Interestingly, many of Mozart's greatest operatic achievements straddle the line, with a story that is clearly comic but an emotional heft that is much more serious.

In addition, for Mozart, there was a German operatic heritage called *singspiel*, which he utilized to its

finest effect in *The Magic Flute*. The idea here is again
fairly obvious, with a form that mixes music with portions of the action that are essentially spoken words.
In a variation of this technique, we might think of much
recitative in a similar manner, although there the narrative continuity is not spoken but declaimed to a musical
accompaniment.

A practice that goes back at least as far as Bach,
whose great Passions include long sections of such nar-
ration, mixed as well with repeated chorales, this technique owes at least a dramatic ancestry to the chorus
in classical Greek plays. Musically, in Mozart, even his
recitative becomes an opportunity to try new combinations of instrument and voice.

IDOMENEO, K. 366, AND DIE ENTFÜHRUNG AUS DEM SERAIL, K. 384

When Mozart set off for Munich late in the year 1780, he
could not have known that the opera *Idomeneo*, which
he had that summer been commissioned to compose,
was about to set in motion a sequence of musical events
that would irrevocably change his life. For him, as always,
the focus was on the work at hand, which in this case
was an opera seria set in Crete after the Trojan War and
telling a strange sort of love story in which Neptune also
plays a part.

It is as if such a nutty story were a mask for what was happening to Mozart, what he was realizing about himself, discovering, resolving, and then finally acting upon. Leopold, a widower since 1778, was still trying to run his son's life. He feared that Mozart might become distracted by romance. He worried that Mozart would not secure the kind of court appointment that would support him and ensure Leopold's own continued support. He wanted as always for his son to succeed, but his perspective, his sense of how success could be defined, was narrow and limiting.

Mozart was feeling frustration over this when he left for Munich. But for one more episode in his life— *Idomeneo*—he was still the dutiful son.

The success of its premiere in Munich two days after his birthday was an enormous confidence boost for someone we think of as not needing one. Mozart eventually returned to Salzburg but soon found himself ordered to Vienna by none other than the hated Archbishop Colloredo, who had been there much of the winter, visiting Mozart's bedridden, sick father. What happened next may have been the single most important decision of Mozart's life.

For reasons about which we can only speculate, the archbishop treated Mozart like a servant, eventually prohibiting him from giving any public performances that would bring in extra income. Finally, things came to a head in early May 1781, when Colloredo ordered Mozart to take a package back to Salzburg for him. Mozart refused and, in a conversation he reported by letter to his father, made a break that presaged the distance he would soon begin to put between himself and Leopold. But the real

MUSINGS ON

George Bernard Shaw on Mozart's gentleness

In the ardent regions where all the rest are excited and vehement, Mozart alone is completely self-possessed: where they are clutching their bars with a grip of iron and forging them with Cyclopean blows, his gentleness of touch never deserts him: he is considerate, economical, practical under the same pressure of inspiration that throws your Titan into convulsions. This is the secret of his unpopularity with Titan fanciers. We all in our native barbarism have a relish for the strenuous: your tenor whose B flat is like the bursting of a boiler always brings down the house, even when the note brutally effaces the song; and the composer who can artistically express in music a transport of vigor and passion of the more muscular kind, such as the finale to the Seventh Symphony, the *Walkürenritt*, or the Hailstone chorus, not to mention the orgies of Raff, Liszt, and Berlioz, is always a hero with the intemperate in music, who are so numerous nowadays that we may confidently expect to see some day a British Minister of the Fine Arts introducing a local Option Bill applied to concert rooms.

---

rupture was within himself; no longer, Mozart was saying, must I do anyone else's bidding:

Archbishop Colloredo: Well, my *lad*, when are you leaving?

Mozart: I wanted to leave tonight but there's no room [on the coach].

With Mozart you are safe from inebriety. Hurry, excitement, eagerness, loss of consideration, are to him purely comic or vicious states of mind: he gives us Monostatos and the Queen of Night on the stage, but not in his chamber music. Now it happens that I have, deep in my nature, which is quite as deep as the average rainfall in England, a frightful contempt for your Queens of Night and Titans and their like. The true Parnassian air acts on these people like oxygen on a mouse: it first excites them, and then kills them. Give me the artist who breathes it like a native, and goes about his work in it as quietly as a common man goes about his ordinary business. Mozart did so; and that is why I like him. Even if I did not, I should pretend to; for a taste for his music is a mark of caste among musicians, and should be worn, like a tall hat, by the amateur who wishes to pass for a true Brahmin.

19 April 1893

As quoted in *Shaw on Music* (1955), edited
by Eric Bently

Colloredo: You are a scoundrel, a scurvy rogue and a cretin.

Mozart: Your grace isn't satisfied with me?

Colloredo: What, are you threatening me, you cretin? Look, there's the door, I want nothing more to do with such a miserable knave.

Mozart: Nor I with you.

Colloredo: Well, go then.

Wow! In this single exchange, reconstructed here from the letter, Mozart has affirmed his response to Polonius's admonition in *Hamlet,* "To thine own self be true," saying in so many words, "I am not a servant. I am Mozart, the composer of numerous symphonies and an opera called *Idomeneo,* and I am a great pianist."

As if to assure his father that things will turn out all right, in the actual letter Mozart added, "I would ask you to be cheerful—my good luck is now beginning, and I hope my good luck will be yours too."

It is a touching finale, because it portends the rift that will develop as the son further declares his independence from the father. And because, as we know, the luck will run out sooner than Mozart might have imagined.

Quickly now, Mozart set down roots in his adopted home. He was already a lodger in the home of the Webers, with whose daughter Aloysia he had once been in love; now he would fall in love with one of her sisters, Constanze, whom he would marry without Leopold's blessing the following summer of 1782, a month after the Viennese premiere of *Die Entführung aus dem Serail.* The new opera, a singspiel that would become his most popular in Vienna during his lifetime, once again was based on an improbable, melodramatic plot, this one set in an Oriental harem.

But neither the story nor its locale really mattered. Something else of much greater importance was taking place, as Mozart was now writing operatic

MUSINGS ON

Placido Domingo
on Idomeneo

Vocally, although Idomeneo is not that easy, it's wonderful. It feels more like a bel canto rather than a typically Mozartian role, probably because the drama of the situation is so intense that you can feel Mozart breaking away from the confines of the strictly "classical" form. In my first aria, "*Vedrommi intorno*," I have just emerged from the sea, I am relieved to be alive but, even before I see that the person approaching me is my son, I grieve for the innocent victim who has to pay for my life with his. Then I have the glorious aria, "*Fuor del mar*," which has the most beautiful music, with quite a lot of coloratura, and although difficult, is marvelous to sing. The Prayer is also very beautiful. The last aria I didn't do; I did only the recitative because that aria was cut from the Met production. These recitatives of Mozart's are among the greatest moments in this opera, the key not only to Idomeneo's but to all the characters' innermost feelings and again, so intense as to seem almost un-Mozartian. . . . One of the most breathtaking moments in this work, however, is the response of the Chorus in Act III, after I reveal that, in order to placate the God, I will have to sacrifice my own son. The music of the chorus in "*O voto tremendo*" is quite incredible, with a modulation going to C major which is just so unbearably poignant and beautiful that, at this moment, you think that there is no composer as simple and as great as Mozart.

From *Placido Domingo: My Operatic Roles* by Helena Matheopoulos, 2003

music free of past convention, with inventive orchestral coloring and gorgeous, soaring, lyrical arias—not on an overall, consistently high level with what was still yet to come, beginning three years later with *The Marriage of Figaro*, but beautifully formed, nevertheless, and deeply felt.

That Mozart did this at a time of such outward conflict is perhaps less surprising than the mysterious flowering of his inner conviction. Why then? Perhaps it was the collision of the two, as if while these outer forces were seemingly wreaking havoc in his life they were really hardening and then activating a new kind of ambition and resolve, the first fruits of which may have been this opera, but the lasting effects of which were to bring forth the most brilliant images and unforgettable creations of the composer we all recognize gratefully as Mozart.

PERHAPS MORE THAN WITH ANY OF Mozart's operas, the most readily available recorded form of *Idomeneo* and *Die Entführung aus dem Serail* seems to be in excerpts. Ilia's aria "Zeffiretti lusinghieri" (Zephyrs caressing) from the former is especially and justifiably popular, while the latter is often represented by the colorful overture and the moving quartet that conclude Act II. But complete recordings of both can be found, including a wonderful 1992 *Entführung* on a DG Archiv double disc, with John Eliot Gardiner leading the Monteverdi Choir and the English Baroque Soloists on authentic instruments and a cast that includes Stanford Olson, Luba Orgonasova, and Cyndia Seiden. With a different cast but the same instrumentalists and choir, Gardiner also recorded *Idomeneo*, again for DG; another fine choice is an EMI recording of Sir Charles Mackerras conducting the Scottish Chamber Orchestra and a cast highlighted by the late Lorraine Hunt Lieberson.

Concert Arias

Much of Mozart's skill in writing for opera singers came from his lifelong experience as a composer of concert arias—single, often extended songs with orchestral accompaniment. He started composing these as a young man and was still at it near the end of his life. All told, he wrote more than four dozen, the majority of which were for sopranos.

These works, occasionally offered one or two at a time in symphonic concerts, can be discovered in several recordings, including an omnibus Decca release of five discs. Some of the other, smaller collections also include selected operatic arias, as if perhaps to remind us that for Mozart the composition of concert arias may also have been a way of "practicing" for his operas.

Concert arias for bass, tenor, and alto round out this less familiar portion of Mozart's oeuvre. They may also inspire listeners to explore some of Mozart's songs, as well. Heaven might be defined as Elisabeth Schwarzkopf's reissued CD of an old EMI mono recording of more than a dozen of the songs, with the great pianist Walter Gieseking accompanying her—no, not accompanying her, playing with her.

In both the songs and the concert arias, take care to note the wide range of keys in which Mozart wrote, in part a concession to his grasp of and empathy for the various talents of the many different singers for whom he wrote so much of this music and whom he clearly held in great affection.

Indeed, part of Mozart's genius is the evident affinity he always felt for the people who would perform the music he composed. Not for Mozart a score that might simply be admired by someone for its architecture and intelligence; and so, like all of his music, his concert arias are first and foremost meant to be heard.

The da Ponte Collaborations

Mozart's break with Archbishop Colloredo and, to a lesser extent, with his father, Leopold, not only signaled a new independence of ambition but also defined an increasing autonomy of resourcefulness. Mozart knew what he wanted to do and confidently found the means within himself. Yet had this singular artist channeled this dual tendency into stubborn self-sufficiency, we might not have inherited the ecstasies and passions of his most superb operatic creations.

But for all his smarts and talents, Mozart, to his great credit—and our eternal gratitude—recognized that there were certain things other artists could do better than he. And so, into his life in 1783 came an Italian writer who would enable Mozart to energize and transform opera

Homage to Mozart à la Donald Baechler for Mostly
Mozart 1995.

in the way that Newton changed physics or Rembrandt
revolutionized portraiture.

Lorenzo da Ponte, as he called himself, was not even
his real name. Seven years Mozart's senior, Emanuele
Conegliano had taken the name of the monsignor who
baptized him as a Catholic, a religion in which he was

preparing to become a priest before ostracizing himself from the authorities in Venice, the city where he lived in his early twenties. Somehow he ended up in Vienna, where Mozart's rival Salieri engaged him as a librettist and helped him secure a theatrical position. Mozart met him at the home of one of his friends, Baron von Plankenstein (who was also for a time Mozart's landlord).

Later, after Mozart's death, da Ponte would move to America, where he would be the proprietor of a grocery store before eventually becoming a professor of Italian at Columbia University. Once he realized how famous his

MUSINGS ON

Aaron Copland
on Mozart's operas

What we expect to find in Mozart is perfection in whatever medium he chose to work. Mozart's operas are no exception, for they embody more resourcefulness than can be found in any other opera up to his time. *The Magic Flute* is sometimes spoken of as the most perfect opera ever written. Its subject matter lends itself very well to operatic treatment because of its nonrealistic nature. It is both serious and comic, combining a wealth of musical imagination with a popular style accessible to all.

One contribution that Mozart did make to the form was the operatic finale. This is an effect possible only in opera—that final scene of an act when all the principals sing at the same time, each one singing about something else, only to conclude with a resounding fortissimo to the delight of

onetime opera collaborator was, he wrote his memoirs, in which he mostly extolled his own role in the three Mozart operas for which he produced the librettos.

Precisely what it was that Mozart recognized in da Ponte when they first met and, two years later, began working together is difficult to decipher. Certainly, one aspect of da Ponte's background, if not personality, that appealed to Mozart was that he was Italian, as Mozart clearly wished to write what he called in a letter to his father an Italian opera. Da Ponte, for his part, must have recognized this in Mozart. He was an intelligent man and obviously a clever one as well and, to judge from what

---

everyone concerned. Mozart accomplished this typically musical trick in so definitive and perfect a way that all who used it after him—as who has not?—were indebted to him. It appears to be a fundamental effect in operatic writing, since it is just as much alive today as it was in Mozart's time.

Mozart was also in advance of his time in one other respect. He was the first great composer to write a comedy set in the German language. *The Abduction from the Seraglio*, produced in 1782, is the first milestone in the path that leads directly to the future German opera. It set the style for a long list of followers, among whom may be counted the Wagner of the *Meistersinger*.

From *Aaron Copland: A Reader: Selected Writings, 1923–1972* (2004)

he produced with Mozart, the kind of writer who could come up with what the composer needed without ever forgetting who was in charge.

That last quality would have been an important one, because for all of Mozart's thoughtfulness toward other

MUSINGS ON *Mozart*

Hector Berlioz on Italian versions of Mozart's operas

I have stated that when I went up for my first examination at the Conservatoire I was wholly absorbed in the study of dramatic music of the grand school; I should have said of lyrical tragedy, and it was owing to this cause that my admiration for Mozart was so lukewarm. Only Gluck and Spontini could excite me. And this was the reason for my coolness with regard to the composer of *Don Giovanni*. *Don Giovanni* and *Figaro* were the two of Mozart's works oftenest played in Paris; but they were always given in Italian, by Italians, at the Italian Opera; and that alone was sufficient to prejudice me against them. Their great defect in my eyes was that they seemed to belong to the ultramontane school. Another and more legitimate objection was a passage in the part of Donna Anna which shocked me greatly, where Mozart has inserted a wretched vocalise which is a perfect blot on his brilliant work. It occurs in the allegro of the soprano aria in the second act, *Non mi dir*, a song of intense sadness, in which all the poetry of love finds vent in lamentation and tear, and which is yet made to wind up with such a ridiculous, unseemly phrase that one wonders how the same man could have written

musicians, he could not have been an easy man to work with. He was very quick, and his technical abilities were so high that any librettist with doubts about his or her talents would have been overwhelmed. Da Ponte's most important characteristic, then, may have been his own self-regard; he was not intimidated by Mozart.

---

both. Donna Anna seems suddenly to have dried her tears and broken out into coarse buffoonery. The words of this passage are, *Forse un giorno il cielo ancora sentira-a-a-a-* (here comes an incredible run, in execrable taste) *pietà di me.* A truly singular form of expression for a noble, outraged woman, of the *hope that heaven will one day have pity on her!* . . . I found it difficult to forgive Mozart for this enormity. Now I feel that I would shed my blood if I could thereby erase that shameful page and others of the same kind which disfigure some of his work. . . .

As I first heard the works of this great composer under such disadvantageous circumstances, it was only many years later that I was able to appreciate their charm and suave perfection. The wonderful beauty of his quartets and quintets, and of some of his sonatas, first converted me to the worship of this angelic genius, whose brightness was slightly dimmed by intercourse with Italian and contrapuntal pedagogues.

From *Memoirs of Hector Berlioz: from 1803 to 1865* (1932)

THE MARRIAGE OF FIGARO, K. 492

In a remarkable long letter to his father on the death of his mother in the summer of 1778, Mozart made brief mention of melancholy, what today we might call the blues. Mozart dealt with the blues on and off through much of his adulthood, demonstrably during the end of his Salzburg era and again toward the last part of his life, beginning sometime in 1788 and ending around 1790 (the year before he died). Even during what was probably the happiest period of his career, the mid-1780s, there was still an omnipresent sense that at any moment things could change for the worse—which, in fact, is the very thing that happened sometime after *The Marriage of Figaro* made its first splash (or was that a thud?) in Vienna in the spring of 1786.

By then, Mozart's days as a concert pianist had pretty much drawn to a close, his relationship with both his hometown public and his patrons was becoming tenuous, and his personal life was, at best, challenging. His father, Leopold, who, as it turned out, had only one more year to live, had never quite succeeded in letting his son go, so that tension between the two never dissipated. Mozart's wife, Constanze, had to make frequent, expensive trips to a spa because of her health. And Mozart's lifestyle, which he supported not only with his concerts and compositions but by taking on pupils, was costing him more than he could afford. Something had to give. But before it did, Mozart in the space of only a couple of years became the finest composer of opera who had ever lived up to then (and, some would say, with the addition of what he did before he died, ever since).

Although none of this information is necessary to appreciate the music of *The Marriage of Figaro* or the opera that followed, *Don Giovanni*, it helps to put the immensity of Mozart's achievement in dramatic human relief. And it ought to give pause to anyone insistent on seeing Mozart's operatic composing as an exercise in musical fairy tales. Much of the plots, both of these two works and one more (*Così fan tutte*) with librettos by da Ponte, are over the top, but they are grounded not only musically but narratively in a conception of life that is at once ambiguous and passionate, as if the composer were simultaneously uncertain and completely confident of love's reasons and intentions.

Love, in fact, is the theme of all three da Ponte collaborations (and of *The Magic Flute*, which came in the last year of Mozart's life). The story of *Figaro* is built around the Count's intention to claim his supposed right to sleep with Figaro's fiancée, Susanna, before Figaro and Susanna are married because they are his servants. Yet as the story unfolds, mistaken recognitions test the validity or foundation of love's faithfulness. In the final act of the opera, mass confusion yields, finally, to a kind of peaceful restoration of order. But the questions the story poses hover over everything, even as the curtain closes.

However, if love were simply the subject or pretext of the plot, *The Marriage of Figaro* might have been not only the first Mozart–da Ponte joint effort but also the last. As always in his career, it is what Mozart did musically with whatever materials he was working with that made all the difference.

In conventional terms, what the typical composer before Mozart would have done with a story like that of *Figaro*—if he had even dared to play with such material—was basically to cross a usually pro forma plot presentation with an assortment of stand-alone arias and a miscellany of other combinations of singers (from duet to chorus). Orchestration, generally speaking, would be in the realm of accompaniment.

Mozart, instead, acting often on what appears to be pure instinct, makes everything of a piece. Plot and characters, recitative and aria, singers and orchestra are integrated; they are all part of an organic whole. The result is not simply a work of enormously entertaining and affecting music but a coherence of form and feeling within an overall aesthetic design that is deeply pleasing and profoundly inspiring. The result, in a word, is what we would call a work of art, in the same way we would use the term to classify creations as otherwise divergent as Proust's *Remembrance of Things Past*, Joyce's *Ulysses*, Picasso's *Guernica*, and Stravinsky's *Rite of Spring*.

All of this, looked at from a modern perspective, may seem obvious, but while Mozart lived and created it was nothing short of revolutionary. Who, his critics and rivals demanded, did Mozart think he was?

Let us fast-forward for just a moment to a rehearsal scene immortalized in the memoirs of the Irish tenor Michael Kelly, an approximate contemporary of Mozart's. The Vienna premier of *The Marriage of Figaro* took place on May 1, 1786, in the city's famed Burgtheater (which is still in use, although it had to be rebuilt after World War II). In those first performances, Michael Kelly sang both of the opera's tenor roles, Don Basilio and Don Curzio.

According to one of Mozart's first biographers, Franz Niemetschek, even the cast of this first *Figaro* production was troubled by the artistic innovations that Mozart's score represented. Whether or not this is true, a moment occurred during the rehearsal of Figaro's aria, "Non più andrai" (From now on), which ends the first act of the four-act opera buffa, that Kelly vividly described in his memoir.

Mozart, Kelly told us, was actually standing onstage at this point, dressed in his usual finery and listening intensely as the Italian baritone Francesco Benucci (Figaro) began to sing.

"I was standing close to Mozart, who, sotto voce," Kelly wrote, "was repeating, 'Bravo! Bravo! Benucci'; and when Benucci came to the fine passage 'Cherubino, alla

A scene from *The Marriage of Figaro*. (H. Montassier)

vittoria, alla gloria militar' [Cherubino, on to glory, on to glory and to fame!] . . . the effect was electricity itself; for the whole of the performers on the stage and those in the orchestra, as if actuated by one feeling of delight, vociferated 'Bravo! Bravo! Maestro, Viva, viva grande Mozart.'" Even the orchestra, Kelly continued, showed its appreciation, in response to which, "The little man acknowledged, by repeated obeisances, the distinguished mark of enthusiastic applause bestowed on him." Bravo!

The scene that Kelly recounted has always been interpreted as evidence of the moment when the cast finally began to grasp the groundbreaking nature of what they were going to perform. This seems quite true, but is not the deeper revelation here what Mozart understood about himself and what he had done?

Accustomed as most of us are to be seated as part of an audience for a performance of a work, the rehearsals for which we certainly were neither invited nor permitted to witness, it may come as a sweet surprise to learn that the musicians themselves invariably have strong opinions about what they are doing. And so this moment that Kelly described underscores our possible lack of knowledge. But even more mysterious to most of us, especially given the fact that the composers of so much of the classical music we hear are long dead, is the reality that they, too, were made of flesh and blood, even the great Bach, the formidable Beethoven, and the endearing Mozart. One could not compose such a piece as *The Marriage of Figaro* without knowing without any quibble or qualification and certainly without false modesty that what you are creating is great.

Well, then, what was it that Mozart created, which so moved those musicians more than two centuries ago?

- an opera buffa in four acts, two of which conclude with glorious, extended finales, something Mozart borrowed from Italian operatic tradition but expanded exponentially;

- a story, based on a play of the same name by the French dramatist Pierre Beaumarchais, which was itself a sequel to a Beaumarchais play that has also inspired an opera (*The Barber of Seville*);

- a sequence of action that takes place entirely within the course of a single day (and that onstage, with intermissions, lasts several hours);

- an opera whose da Ponte libretto, like the Beaumarchais play, ridicules the nobility, though less so than did the play (which caused many uproars and was frequently censored and in some instances was prohibited from being performed);

- an opera whose apparent central focus is on the marriage of its lead characters, a servant named Figaro and his fiancée, Susanna, a maid to the wife of Figaro's boss, the duplicitous Count Almaviva;

- an opera whose apparent incidental focus on such secondary characters as the count's music master, Don Basilio, or even Barbarina, the daughter of the count's gardener, Antonio, not only buttresses the primary story line but also at several memorable musical times dares to question what were (and still for many are) traditional notions of social importance;

- an opera whose music, from the overture (which, as was always the case with Mozart, was the last thing he wrote) to the final call to celebrate ("Ah! tutti contenti saremo così"[We are all happy and contented again]), never flags, and usually in fact soars, even in the recitatives;

- an opera that after its first Viennese performance was repeated during its initial run only eight more times to a public that was mixed in its reception, but which then came to Prague at the end of 1786;

- an opera that was so popular in Prague that Mozart was invited to come to that city, which he not only did but ended up conducting some of the performances there, during a visit in which he also presented his thirty-eighth symphony, which came to be known as the *Prague*, and a visit that produced a commission for *Don Giovanni*, the opera that would follow; and,

- an opera that, like *Don Giovanni,* has never left the basic operatic repertory and is today performed again and again around the world.

A roster of Mozart's greatest hits could be put together simply from *The Marriage of Figaro.* No doubt, some opera lovers would deem this a heresy, but it is more than possible to listen to this opera in a state of suspended, ecstatic animation without really knowing the story, let alone the meaning of the language. Take, for example, the brief, beautiful cavatina with which Barbarina opens the fourth and final act. She laments:

L'ho perduta, me meschina!
Ah! chi sa dove sarà?
E mia cugina,
E il padron cosa dirà?

I have lost it,
Heaven help me,
I have lost the little pin.
What will my cousin and the count say!

Imagine, such sorrow over such a seeming trifle, though one that matters at that moment to the drama. But it matters to us even more—because of the music, which in real time lasts all of a minute and three quarters but in our memories may linger forever. Talking about anything like this runs such a risk of hyperbole, but there must be many accomplished composers who never once in their successful careers reached such lyrical height and emotional depth, and Mozart does it in *Figaro* at least two dozen times.

AN IMPOSSIBLY DELICIOUS ASSIGNMENT awaits anyone choosing a favorite recording of what for many people is their favorite opera. Among the wide array of choices, a terrific recent Harmonia Mundi recording finds the Mozart specialist René Jacobs leading the Concerto Köln, with a cast that includes Lorenzo Regazzo as Figaro, Patrizia Ciofi as Susanna, Simon Keenlyside as the Count, and Véronique Gens as the Countess. The redoubtable Sir Charles Mackerras conducts the Scottish Chamber Orchestra and Chorus in a 1994 Telarc recording that is usually available at a budget price; cast members include the great Carol Vaness as the Countess.

Among historic recordings still available are maestro Karl Böhm's 1966 Salzburg Festival production with Walter Berry as Figaro (this recording comes as a black-and-white Telarc DVD) and a Deutsche Grammophon recording with the German Opera and Chorus that features the luminescent baritone Dietrich Fischer-Dieskau as the Count. Also superb is Erich Kleiber's Decca recording from half a century ago and a later Decca recording, for many people their first choice, with Sir Georg Solti leading the London Philharmonic Orchestra and Chorus with an all-star cast of Samuel Ramey as Figaro, Lucia Popp as Susanna, Thomas Allen as the Count, Kiri Te Kanawa as the Countess, and Frederica von Stade as Cherubino.

DON GIOVANNI, K. 527

In one of his own many letters, the poet John Keats, whose life was even shorter than Mozart's, articulated a concept that he called "negative capability." The basic idea, which Keats believed was intrinsic to the poet's ability to write great poetry, is to hold simultaneously two thoughts or feelings that are in opposition to each other. This was certainly something Mozart understood, never more clearly or powerfully than in his magnum opus, *Don Giovanni*.

Somewhat to Mozart's surprise, because he and da Ponte in their *Marriage of Figaro* had toned down some of the antagonism toward the nobility that animated the Beaumarchais play, Mozart's adoring Viennese public began to leave him after that opera's 1786 performances. It was around that time that Mozart had also found the audience for his piano concertos shrinking, either because of displeasure with the composer of *Figaro* or simply because people and their tastes are fickle.

And so Mozart was especially buoyed when he was invited in early 1787 to Prague, where a production of *Figaro* was a huge hit. He returned to Vienna from that visit with a commission for a new opera and perhaps as well with a somewhat chastened—or should that be newly sharpened?—appreciation for human nature.

Through its depiction of a libertine and his downfall, the story of *Don Giovanni* poses a troubling question about human behavior. But the music provides more than a sonic complement or, on the other hand, a simple response, let alone answer. Mozart's music in this opera *is* both the question and the answer, the pain and the pleasure, the sadness and the joy. Life, the music says, even operatic life, is at least that complicated. And so, in this endlessly inquisitive and affirming opera buffa, there is never a mere breaking down of basic dualities.

It is terribly tempting to wonder about the wealth of experience that brought Mozart to a full sense of the enormous potential to do good or evil harbored within each of us. But we have, really, only his correspondence and that of a few others to go on, and by the time of *Don Giovanni* very little even of those resources from which to glean information, if not insight.

Realistically, however, can the experience of an artist of Mozart's caliber and range be reduced to a quantum of fact and detail? Is there not something inherently absurd about the basis of such a proposition? We might just as well try to "explain" the meaning of a spring morning, a howling wind, a mother's embrace, a child's cry, a robin's flight . . . the beauty of a man or a woman.

Working with a libretto that da Ponte based on numerous different dramatic treatments of the Don Juan legend or archetype, Mozart composed an opera that simultaneously

Don Giovanni. His story poses a troubling question about
human behavior. (H. Montassier)

soars and sears with the double-edged sword of desire.
To what extent the composer's perception of passion
transmutes or transposes his own personal vision pales in
comparison to the achievement of the music in convey-
ing the multiplicity of emotions that are both cause and
effect of Don Giovanni's licentiousness.

Mozart pulled this off by writing music that is at
once a dramatic realization of character and plot and an
apparent foil for the very emotion one would expect.
At a moment of perfidy, he gave Don Giovanni a lyric

of breadth and depth; at another of pathos, he added a comedic element that at first undercuts the tension but then, lingering, broadens it.

Very little is known about how Mozart and da Ponte worked this all out, though the scant evidence does at least suggest that they remained partners throughout, with da Ponte expressing some amazement later at the degree to which Mozart had extended da Ponte's central conception of the story—pushed the envelope, in today's vernacular.

There are many moments in this long opera when the two collaborators could have taken the easy way out, milking the situation for false sentiment. That never happens. Instead, working through the spring and the summer of 1787, they shaped and sharpened a story whose denouement is one of the most overwhelming in all opera. Don Giovanni, given a last chance to change his ways, refuses and disappears into hell.

That descent, foreordained by the ominous, opening chords of the opera—such drama! such tension!—brings us immediately into the opera's world, a world of words and costumes and scenery and acting and music—most of all, music. Not the least of this opera's amazements is the unflagging nature of the music: its forward motion envelops us from the very beginning and then never really pauses, certainly never actually stops. Mozart did this by using every technique he had learned not only in his previous operas but in so much of the other music he had written beforehand: *Don Giovanni* is the work not only of a great artist but also of a master craftsman. Note, for example, how integral the orchestra is to everything that happens onstage, almost as if the orchestra itself were a collective character in the cast.

MUSINGS ON

Mozart

Ned Rorem on Mozart's "gift
to be simple"

Awestruck by Mozart, people ask how he made magic from
mere scales, and they cite the slow ebbing strings at the
climax of *Don Giovanni*. Then they proffer their own non-
answer: He was Mozart!

A real answer: Assuming the strings are magic, they are
not "mere" scales. Mere scales are just that, mere, and
get boring in lesser Mozart sonatas. However, in his opera
the composer does turn a seven-note melodic minor mode
into two (ascending, then descending) eight-note harmonic
minor passages. He immediately repeats this pattern a half-
tone higher, then a whole tone higher, and so on up chromat-
ically, ever tightening the screw with this pseudomodulatory
device (or vise) much copied in today's pop songs. Meanwhile
a human basso intones a pedal "A" whose color alters
according to the flux of color beneath, above, and beside it.
These independent occurrences are melded by "abstract"
chords of sustained lower brass, by a kettledrum heartbeat,

The apparent ease with which Mozart achieved this
belies the tremendous labor the composition of this opera
must have entailed—and which its modern production
today requires. Singers are stretched to their utmost, not
only the two sopranos who play Donna Anna and Donna
Elvira but also the baritone who plays Don Giovanni—how
Mozart loved baritones, too—and Don Ottavio, a tenor;
Don Giovanni's servant Leporello and Donna Anna's father,
Il Commendatore (the Commandant), both basses; and the
smaller parts of Masetto, a tenor, and Zerlina, a soprano.

and by the Commendatore's "concrete" language. Now, this concrete language—Italian prose—is missing from Mozart's first and only "plant" of the menacing mood, hours earlier, in the overture. But because the plant hints to connoisseurs what is to come (though the curtain's not yet up and human voices haven't yet been introduced), the scales in the overture may justly be termed psychological, a word inappropriate to any wholly nonvocal music, including Beethoven's quartets.

Mozart's "mere" scale was but one of many simultaneous happenings on this page: we may be aware of just that scale while the rest is subliminal; but that rest, while maybe magic, is analyzable magic.

That paragraph voices but one of many warnings about oversimplifying the gift to be simple. It's hard to be easy. Simplicity results from complex tailorings.

From *Settling the Score: Essays on Music* (1988)

The action begins with Don Giovanni's murder of the Commandant, who has tried to save his daughter from Don Giovanni's clutches in a scene that takes place outside the Commandant's castle. Relentlessly, the story continues through this first of just two acts as the other characters are introduced and Don Giovanni's designs are finally focused on a young woman named Zerlina, who is married to the peasant Masetto.

With plot twists that include a character (in this case, Leporello) disguised as another (Don Giovanni)—a

MUSINGS ON

Sherrill Milnes on performing Don Giovanni

The performances were in the old Masonic Temple in Detroit. The dressing rooms were upstairs, small, tawdry, and ill-equipped—usual for old theaters. Late in the opera, during the second act sextet, I have about twenty minutes to wait for my next entrance. With loudspeakers in the rooms, I could hear exactly where everyone was. I went to the bathroom and closed the door behind me. When I went to open the door, the knob spun in my hand, and the door would not open. I pushed and wiggled the door with all my force, but nothing happened. I called out and banged on the door and still nothing happened. Then I realized that all my colleagues were onstage and my dressing room was located off in a corner, so no one was close enough to be able to hear. I could hear my entrance music coming closer and there seemed to be nothing I could do. I don't think I had ever been in that situation before. I yelled and banged on the door some more, but to no avail. The entrance cue was coming closer.

---

veritable staple of any da Ponte-Mozart partnership—the second act builds inexorably toward that final terrifying scene, when the Commandant appears as a statue, a ghost in stone. The action concludes with a kind of postscript, not always performed, in which the other characters declaim in song their view of Don Giovanni's end. "Resti dunque quel birbon / Con Proserpina e Pluton!" sing Zerlina, Masetto, and Leporello. (Leave the rascal lying, then, / Safely shut in Pluto's den.) They are joined by Donna Anna, Donna Elvira, and Don Ottavio:

I saw that the center of the door was made of thinner plywood than the outside portion. Giovanni wears boots with heavy soles and heels, so I used them to try to kick out the plywood section of the door. Even though it was thinner, it still took some doing, but finally I splintered enough wood to make an opening. I continued to kick and smash the wood until I made a big enough hole to push myself through and clear the door. As I ran to the stage, I looked back to see the mess I had made of the door, chuckled to myself, and arrived just in time to sing my first recitative lines of the graveyard scene. Fortunately, Giovanni is supposed to be out of breath and excited when he enters, and I certainly was. Maybe my bathroom escape added some extra dimension to the scene; I didn't know and at that moment, I didn't care. The audience was none the wiser.

From *American Aria: From Farm Boy to Opera Star* (1998)

So do all deceivers end, deceivers end,
So they end, all deceivers end.
So do all wrongdoers end,
Wrongdoers end, wrongdoers end.
Rakes, betrayers, all take warning
While there's time (while there's time)
still your ways to mend.
Your ways to mend.
Mend your ways.

MUSINGS ON

Hao Jiang Tian on playing the Commendatore in *Don Giovanni*

Just shy of thirteen years of age, I witnessed a suicide during the early years of the Cultural Revolution.

The man lay at the base of the tall pagoda from which he had jumped. The suggestion of a smile would not leave my mind. It never will. And though I could do nothing to help this man in his final moments in 1967 in Beijing, remarkably he came to my rescue in 1995 in Bonn, where I was performing in Mozart's *Don Giovanni* for the first time and dying—in more ways than one—in a staging rehearsal. The Italian director, famous in theater but never having worked in opera, marched onto the stage briskly—"*Buon giorno!*"— flipped a chair around, sat down, stuck a pipe in his mouth, and puffed a big cloud of smoke. I was singing the role of the Commendatore, who is murdered by Don Giovanni in the first scene of the first act. I hadn't a clue how to act this part, so I was eager to hear the kind of guidance I'd come to expect in opera: where to stand, what to do, how to appear.

"Okay, let's start." That's all he said. This was the first time I'd worked with a director who didn't direct!

I was on my own. What was I to do? I die in this very first scene at the hands of the proud, boastful man who has tried to have his way with my daughter, whose honor I'm now trying to defend. But how? Then it came to me, that pale face, that sweet almost-smile from the poor man dying in the Summer Palace. He whispered to me, "I am hurt. I am dying, but I am relieved of pain." I thought, "I am hurt, and I am dying, but I know I have given my life for my daughter's honor and I die in peace, relieved of my pain." So almost in slow motion I slumped to the stage, peacefully, with relief, and with the suggestion of a smile.

"Bravo!" called the director, jumping from his chair and running to me as I stood back up. He grabbed me by the shoulders and insisted I tell him how I came up with that move. So I told him about that summer day in the Summer Palace nearly thirty years before when the man jumped to his death. The director was silent. When the pipe smoke cleared around his face, he looked sad. Then a big smile spread over his face.

"You understand me," he said. Turning to the rest of the cast, he said, "That's what I'm looking for. Find what works for you and if I like it, we'll go with that."

I blessed that man in the Summer Palace whose name I never knew but whose death, I hoped, I had found some way to honor.

From *Along the Roaring River: My Wild Ride from Mao to the Met* (written with Lois B. Morris, 2008)

Despite that moral, operagoers in Mozart's day were not necessarily placated, especially those whose purview it was to decide what should be presented where and how often. Only in Prague, where the opera was premiered in November 1787, did *Don Giovanni* find an immediate public during Mozart's lifetime. When the opera was produced in Vienna during the following year (with changes in the score that still trigger debate), it was respectfully received but hardly the headliner it would eventually become, performed now by opera companies everywhere and universally recognized as a masterpiece.

To list all of the reasons that is so would be to replicate here the entire score, brimming as it is with aria after chorus after recitative after duet and trio—and even a stunning sextet near the beginning of Act II. Among the many first-act highlights are Leporello's aria "Madamina, il catalogo è questo" (also known as "The Catalogue Aria"); the duet between Don Giovanni and Zerlina, "Là ci darem la mano" (There we'll be hand in hand, dear); Don Ottavio's aria "Dalla sua pace"(On her peace of mind); and the thrilling first finale. In the second act, in addition to the sextet, Don Ottavio has another aria,"Il mio tesoro intanto andate a consolar"(Meantime go and console my dearest one); Donna Elvira sings,"Mi tradi quell' alma ingrata"; and Donna Anna breaks all hearts with a kind of recitative,"Crudele! Ah no!" that is immediately followed by one of the most beautiful arias in all of Mozart, "Non mi dir, bell'idol mio" (Say not, my beloved).

Composer and librettist both are on the highest plane there, in a lyric later interpreted by the late poet W. H. Auden, working with Chester Kallman:

Let yonder moon, chaste eye of Heaven
Cool desire and calm your soul;
May the bright stars their patience lend you.
As their constellations roll,
Turn, turn, turn about the Pole.
Far, too far they seem from our dying,
Cold, we call them, to our sighing;
We, too proud, too evil-minded,
By sin are blinded.

No doubt for some of the people in the opera's first audiences, as well as many of those who have followed, the difficulty or challenge of *Don Giovanni* is the very thing that makes it so great: how to square such extraordinarily gorgeous music with a story that depicts human behavior at its most vile. For Mozart, however, this was apparently not a test at all; rather, his triumph here is the reconciliation of what appear to be the contradictory forces of life and art. They are, in *Don Giovanni* as they were in the great tragedies of Shakespeare or, later, the immortal odes of Keats, *one*.

IT SHOULD COME AS NO SURPRISE THAT the discography for *Don Giovanni* is a kind of history of great singers, conductors, and orchestras from years ago right up to now. Truly, they give meaning to the old phrase "an embarrassment of riches."

If you can find it, there may be no better recording of the opera than that of Josef Krips leading the Vienna Philharmonic Orchestra and an all-star cast of singers who, sadly, have like Krips disappeared from the scene (the Decca recording was made more than fifty years ago). Also among the heavyweights from a bygone era are Wilhelm Furtwängler's EMI recording, with the same Vienna Philharmonic Orchestra and a cast that again includes the great bass Cesare Siepi and the soprano Elisabeth Schwarzkopf—both of whom also appear on yet another Furtwängler recording of the opera, this one for Orfeo, again with the same orchestra. Schwarzkopf, as well as Joan Sutherland, stars on the remastered EMI recording from 1959 led by Carlo Maria Giulini with the Philharmonia Orchestra and Chorus.

Recent recordings include a fine Decca release, made in 2006 at the Salzburg Festival and available on DVD. The exemplary baritone Thomas Hampson sings the title role, once again with the Vienna Philharmonic Orchestra, which must have a patent on this piece, this time led by maestro Daniel Harding. Rodney Gilfry is Don Giovanni in John Eliot Gardiner's fine Deutsche Grammophon recording with the Monteverdi Choir and the English Baroque Orchestra. As on Gardiner's other magnificent Mozart recordings, his orchestra here consists of musicians playing period instruments.

COSÌ FAN TUTTE, K. 588

Soave sia il vento,
tranquilla sia l'onda,
ed ogni elemento
benigno risponda
ai nostri desir!

May the wind be gentle,
may the sea be calm,
and may the elements
respond kindly
to our wishes.

So sing the two sisters, Fiordiligi and Dorabella, along with the supposedly trustworthy Don Alfonso, "an old philosopher," in a fairly early scene in the first act of the two-act da Ponte-Mozart opera *Così fan tutte*. The scene itself, like everything in this 1790 opera buffa, is a setup. Ostensibly, the men whom the two women are supposedly going to marry—Guglielmo and Ferrando—are off to do their military service. In fact, they are part of a wager with Don Alfonso, who has insisted that the sisters will forget their true loves once they are gone. And so we have this forced farewell, in which Don Alfonso is playing along with a situation in which we in the audience are to believe that Fiordiligi and Dorabella are genuinely sorrowful at the departure of their lovers.

Well, who could not believe with them, listening to the music?

Mozart tries every trick here. He is veritably diabolical! And he will do it again and again in this last collaboration with da Ponte, whose libretto, from all we know, was based on an original story.

But story is hardly the point. Rather, it is a mere vehicle for getting us to the gist of the emotion in each scene, each aria. This opera, which includes some of the most beautiful music ever written by anyone, is never meant to be taken seriously—except, of course, when "breezes blow lightly." Which they often do.

For many years, the basic plot of *Così fan tutte* was considered shocking, even immoral, by audiences. Were we really to believe that women would so easily overlook their allegiances and pledges . . . and then, on the denouement, be forgiven? For in the plot's resolution, after the two men first return—in a disguise that only the two sisters do not recognize—and each successfully woos the other's fiancée, only to have the truth finally come out, all is eventually pardoned. Can Mozart and da Ponte be this facile? Of course not.

Let us return to that farewell that the trio sings. A harpsichord strikes a single chord. The strings come, playing a figure within triads, and then the heavenly melody begins. The contrast, the opposition between the two—like the competing emotions in any lover's heart—is at once unbearably tense and poignantly affecting. And so, as the strings continue their ascent and descent while the melody itself begins to soar, we are totally seduced—just as the sisters in the actual story have been. But, listening, we are less concerned with *them* than with the *music,* which, as if a miracle were taking place, we suddenly sense is tracing something in the trajectory of our own longings and losses. And so we, like the sisters, succumb.

This sort of sorcery happens often in *Così*, which is perhaps why, now, it is one of Mozart's most frequently performed operas. Much of it is funny and endearing: we see ourselves onstage, hear our whispers and wishes. Much of it, too, seems a foil for Mozart's earlier great opera about love, *The Marriage of Figaro*. Similarly in *Così fan tutte*, mistaken identities and plot twists test the validity or foundation of love, except in this case the plot twists are clearly farcical. Even the costume changes that accompany the temporary taking of new identities are a joke that the audience is in on from the start. Were that the end of the story, *Così* would be considered little more than a comedy of manners set to music. Something else, however—something much grander, much more profound—is going on.

Mozart's grandest motive is, of course, the music. Let's return again to that trio from the first act, with its melody that would melt any heart and an orchestral scoring that makes the orchestra part of the cast, really—a musical conceit that Mozart has employed many times before and not only in opera. Think, for example, of the part the orchestra plays in his finest piano concertos. Piano and orchestra are forever intertwined; like concerto, like opera.

Over and over in *Così fan tutte*, Mozart repeats this trick. Except he's not joking with us here; there is no ploy, no deception, unless we think of the entire ridiculous story as such. But Mozart never condescends to the libretto; always, his music takes seriously the libretto's *aim*—it is why, beyond its beauty, we pay attention.

Take another great moment, although *moment* is a poor choice of word; even *place* seems incorrect, unless we mean the space that the particular passage creates, space in the opera, space in our sense of the opera . . . space in our lives.

We are nearing but not yet at the midpoint of the second act. Ferrando and Guglielmo in disguise are vying for the affections of the sisters, each wooing the fiancée of the other. Dorabella, engaged to Ferrando, seems to be succumbing to Guglielmo, but Fiordiligi is trying mightily to resist the imploring of Ferrando. Tormented by the realization that she was at least tempted to betray her true love, Guglielmo, she questions herself in a solo recitative, what in a play we would call a soliloquy.

And then, immediately, she launches into the most extraordinary aria that Mozart has not only written in the form of, but even identified as, a rondo. She sings:

Per pietà, ben mio, perdona
all'error d'un alma amante.

Dearest love, I beg your pardon
For the faith that I have broken.

Slowly at first and then with an almost imperceptible quickening of the tempo, Mozart returns to the musical figure that begins this passage—thus its classification as a rondo. The orchestra weeps with Fiordiligi as she pours out her anguish. Little by little, the dynamic of both singer and orchestra builds with her repeated plea; it is almost as if, by making this declaration, she has bolstered her confidence in herself and we can hear that in the assertiveness of the music. Incrementally, too, the line of the lyric rises as the soprano singing the part of Fiordiligi is put through increasingly difficult paces, the notes going higher and with coloratura flourishes that Mozart bestows as if they were a gift of precious gems.

And then another jewel: an ascending series of short arpeggios played by the violins, repeated, all while Fiordiligi moves now toward the climax of her aria, "Caro bene, al tuo candor" (For my fault I shall atone), and we listen, spellbound, barely able to breathe, until our own tears finally come.

One is reminded here of another composer's exhortation, well into the next century after Mozart's death.

Hector Berlioz, concluding his mammoth *Memoirs*, recounts his reunion with a woman whom he had loved years before. Amazingly, in a development we can barely believe but that would have made for good da Ponte libretto material, her name is Stella, a name that comes from the Latin word for "star." "And here I end," Berlioz wrote, in Ernest Newman's translation. "I can live more peacefully now. I shall sometimes write to her; she will answer me. I shall go and see her. . . . My sky is not without its star." Finally, in a refrain that is unmistakably French, he asks what is greater, love or music? "Love," he says, answering his own impossible question, "can give no idea of music; music can give an idea of love. . . . Why separate them? They are the two wings of the soul."

"The soul, or the sword?" Mozart might rejoin. Despite the happy ending of *Così fan tutte*, in which the lovers are reunited, Mozart seemed forever aware of the temporality that all but the most profound love may possess. And he conveyed this not in words but in the music. Fiordiligi's plaintive cry is more than a plea for forgiveness. We hear in her hushed wail and the undercurrent of tension created by the harmonic interaction of the orchestra with her melody a cry that extends far beyond the particular story that *Così fan tutte* tells. In another of the second act's aria, Fiordiligi's sister, Dorabella, explains:

È amore un ladroncello,
un serpentello è amor

Love's a little thief
a little serpent is love.

FOR AN OPERA FILLED WITH AS MANY gorgeous arias and such a stunning orchestral score as *Così fan tutte*, a long list of singers and conductors who have recorded it awaits the lucky opera fan. Certainly near or at the top of that list is the long-time artistic director of New York's Metropolitan Opera Company, James Levine, whose live presentations of any Mozart opera—even with a student orchestra at Tanglewood—are command performances.

Maestro Levine's 1989 Deutsche Grammophon (DG) interpretation of *Così fan tutte* is stellar, with a cast that includes Kiri Te Kanawa and Thomas Hampson. The orchestra is the Vienna Philharmonic.

Time was, and not that long ago, that people thought Mozart had to be performed by such groups as the Vienna Philharmonic Orchestra. Happily, that old prejudice has died. Groups such as the English Baroque Orchestra—here, in *Così*, again led by John Eliot Gardiner on a DG recording (also available on DVD)—continue to excel in modern Mozart (although this group, as is its engaging custom, plays on period instruments). Sir Simon Rattle, originally of Birmingham fame and more recently the music director of the Berlin Philharmonic, conducts the Orchestra of the Age of Enlightenment in an EMI recording with a fine cast. The recording was made in the stunning Symphony Hall in Birmingham, built while Rattle ran the show there, and this adds a further acoustical sheen to the sound.

Other *Così* conductors to be on the lookout for are Sir Georg Solti (with Renée Fleming as Fiordiligi and Anne Sophie von Otter as Dorabella) and Karl Böhm, both of whom boast a discography that includes more than one recording of the opera. A highlight of Solti's with the London Philharmonic Orchestra is the singing of Pilar Lorengar as Fiordiligi, although it would be hard to trump Elisabeth Schwarzkopf in the same role on Böhm's recording with the Philharmonia Chorus and Orchestra and also featuring Christa Ludwig singing the part of Dorabella. Miah Persson, Christine Rice, and Bryn Terfel shine with the Scottish Chamber Orchestra under Sir Charles Mackerras on a Mozart highlights disc that includes an incandescent "Soave sia il vento." Mackerras, who recorded the complete *Così* with the same ensemble but different soloists, also made a Telarc recording of *Così* with the Edinburgh Festival Choir and Orchestra, available as well on a highlights disc, and yet another with the Orchestra of the Age of Enlightenment: a busy man!

ENCHANTMENT: *THE MAGIC FLUTE*, K. 620

There are two ways a person can choose to listen to the final Mozart operatic masterpiece. You can try to make sense of the implausible story and connect it with the music, or you can simply enjoy the music and think of the story as a kind of fairy tale and a very improbable one at that.

By the time Mozart received the commission to write *Die Zauberflöte* (The Magic Flute), his fortunes were beginning to change for the better. After a prolonged period of financial and personal struggle in the late 1780s, during which he frequently had to borrow money, Mozart had seemingly turned the corner with the successful premiere of *Così fan tutte* in early 1790.

But the death of that opera's patron, Emperor Joseph II, put a stop to its performances and, temporarily, to the improvement of Mozart's circumstances.

Through the next year, into early 1791, Mozart failed to improve his court position under the new emperor and even, some experts think, considered following his friend and champion, the older composer Haydn, to London. He wrote his last two string quintets and his last piano concerto. Constanze, in and out of the spa at Baden, was pregnant and in July would give birth to a son, the second of the couple's children to survive. But before that date, sometime in the spring of 1791, Mozart had started working on a new opera, a singspiel, with a German libretto by an old family friend, Emanuel Schikaneder, who ran a successful theater company in the outskirts of

La clemenza di Tito

By some accounts, Mozart composed this finale in his operatic oeuvre, K. 621, in a mere eighteen days. More likely, he stole some of the time during the summer of 1791 when he was composing *The Magic Flute* to work on this as well, having received the commission for it then. Whatever the case, he stopped work on *The Magic Flute* in August and headed to Prague, where he stayed until the early September performance of an opera that has never been a great favorite, either because he spent so little time on it or, simply, because his heart wasn't really in it.

That said, there are some stirring, Mozartean moments in *La clemenza di Tito*, with a libretto by a writer named Metastasio, who had already served such luminaries as Cristoph Willibald Gluck. Salieri, so the story goes, had declined the commission, which was part of the festivities surrounding the coronation of Leopold II as emperor of what was then called Bavaria.

The libretto's story focuses on an ancient intrigue of love and betrayal in which a ruler named Tito eventually absolves a man named Publio and his fellow conspirators of their role in a plot to burn the capital and kill him (Tito). The infrequently performed opera has been notably recorded by René Jacobs leading the esteemed Freiburg Baroque Orchestra. Sir Charles Mackerras has also made a recording with his beloved Scottish Chamber Orchestra, and so, among others, has John Eliot Gardiner with the Monteverdi Choir and the English Baroque Orchestra. For Mozart addicts only.

Vienna. It was Schikaneder's idea to base the story on an Oriental fairy tale, but to this both men added elements of Freemasonry, popular at this time among European intellectuals, including both Mozart and Schikaneder. What came out of this last major collaboration in Mozart's career ought to color our perception of the end of Mozart's life at least as much as the legend of the Requiem.

The two men worked together through that summer, when Mozart's labors were interrupted by yet another opera commission, this on the occasion of the September coronation of Leopold II. Not until after that event, held in Prague, did Mozart return to Vienna and complete the music for the opera. The premiere, with the composer on the podium as conductor, took place on September 30 at Schikaneder's Theater auf der Wieden. The audience was enthusiastic, and word quickly spread within the city; soon, long lines formed each night outside the theater as people vied for coveted tickets. Surely, the occasion must have been one of the happiest of Mozart's life, which was to end in only two months.

Like the three operas on which Mozart collaborated with da Ponte—who was banished to America by the new emperor—*The Magic Flute* takes love as its central subject. But there the similarity ends. Whereas the da Ponte operas all focused on individual characters, the figures in *The Magic Flute* are types, human symbols used to represent universal themes of brotherhood, justice, freedom.

Two sets of lovers focus our attention in a plot that may be the most convoluted in all of opera. The handsome Tamino, having been rescued by three mysterious ladies from the attack of a serpent, sees a picture of the beautiful Pamina, the daughter of the Queen of the Night. At first, we are led to believe that the Queen is good, but we shall soon be disabused of that thought. Before then, however, the Queen has sent Tamino on a rescue mission to find Pamina, who she reports has been taken away from the supposedly evil Sarastro. We will eventually come to see him in a different light.

First, however, we encounter Papageno, a bird-catcher who lives in the forest and who, after initially trying to take credit for saving Tamino, is enlisted to help Tamino in his search. They are aided by two magic instruments given

MUSINGS ON

Renée Fleming on Mozart as gentle teacher

Frankly, I would have chosen Berio, Puccini, Berlioz, or Stravinsky—anything but Mozart—as my introduction to the international stages of the world. While I would have preferred to avoid having to live up to his requirement of crystal-clear, naked perfection, in retrospect I'm grateful for that repertoire, as it helped protect my voice. I had no choice but to sing well and carefully for that first decade of my career, maintaining a youthful weight and quality to my voice, when the demands of other composers—full-voiced drama over a heavy orchestra—would have used me up by now, and I'd likely be hearing from opera companies, "Thank you very much, but you have a wobble and your top isn't what it used to be." Sheer luck again sent me into Mozart's demanding but safe hands.

From *The Inner Voice: The Making of a Singer* (2004)

---

to them by the three ladies: a glockenspiel for Papageno and—can you guess?—a magic flute for Tamino!

Confused? Fear not; at this point in the plot we are barely under way. Ahead are permutations upon transformations upon variations as Papageno encounters the Moor Monostatos; a first momentous meeting takes place between Tamino and Pamina; and three boys are introduced (they will play a key role in the action to come, a good deal of which turns on the purposes of Sarastro, a priest whose temples Tamino stumbles upon). Ahead, too, Papageno will meet his beloved Papagena, at first with her in the person of an old woman.

By then, Tamino will have been tested three times, the last with Pamina by his side, in order to prove his worthiness to marry her. His trials include the injunction not to speak, which of course leads to consternation on the part of Pamina. He must also make his way through fire and water as he and Pamina walk together through a mountain. Somehow they make it through, aided by the magic flute,

MUSINGS ON

Daniel Barenboim on his first encounter with a Mozart opera

My curiosity was naturally tremendous, and I saw that the performance that evening [in Salzburg] was to be *Die Zauberflöte*, conducted by Karl Böhm. I had never been to the opera, and was terribly excited and wanted to go in. It was, of course, impossible to get tickets, but I said to my mother that I thought I could slip in the public gallery without a ticket—I was a small boy, only nine years old, and nobody would take any notice. But I did not know where to find my parents afterwards, because they were obviously much too law-abiding even to try to get in without tickets, so they looked around and told me that they would wait for me in Café Tomaselli, which is within walking distance of the Festspielhaus. Hiding myself in the middle of the crowd where nobody would notice me, I waited till we all seemed to be in and then opened a door which fortunately led to an empty box. Sitting down very comfortably, and feeling extremely happy and proud of myself for having managed to get in without a ticket, I waited impatiently for the conductor to start the performance. As soon as he did I was

which we learn was fashioned by Pamina's father from the wood of an oak tree a thousand years old.

A final challenge to the couple's happiness comes from the Queen of the Night and Monostatos, but Sarastro prevails, the sun comes out, and all is well. Good has triumphed over evil.

From a purely theatrical standpoint, the story begs for

---

overjoyed; there was applause and the overture started. I remember perhaps about ten or twenty bars—I suppose that thereafter total exhaustion from the trip overwhelmed me and the excitement was just too much—for I promptly fell asleep and did not hear a note of either the rest of the overture or the singing or dialogue that followed.

The next thing I remember is waking up and suddenly being terribly frightened. I had no idea where I was, I heard music being playing and everybody was sitting down, and for a second I could not remember where my parents were or what I was doing there, so far from any familiar surroundings. I started crying very loudly, whereupon the usher came and very firmly, if not brutally, took me out of the box where I was disturbing the public, and threw me out of the Festspielhaus. Then, of course, I remembered that my parents were at the Café Tomaselli and went to join them, still crying. . . . That was my first encounter with a Mozart opera, which obviously did not augur very well for the future!

From *A Life in Music* (2003)

Costume and set designs for *The Magic Flute*. (Engravings by
the Schaffer brothers)

scenery and costuming that make the opera into a true
spectacle, which was no doubt one reason for its initial
popularity and which still adds crowd-pleasing elements
of dramatic stagecraft. A fully mounted production of *The
Magic Flute* is among the greatest pleasures an operagoer
can enjoy, and even a shortened version of the opera in
the right hands can be a success—witness Julie Taymor's
sparkling holiday reduction for families at the Metropolitan Opera in New York.

It is the music, however, that carries the show, letting
us forget not; only the plot complications but also the
difficulties of our own lives. Musicians and audiences
alike can debate whether *The Magic Flute* is Mozart's
best opera—the smart money is still on *Don Giovanni*,

although both *The Marriage of Figaro* and *Così fan tutte* also have their passionate adherents. But who is taking a poll? Building with many musical materials that he did not use before, Mozart in *The Magic Flute* managed to combine the ingredients of this operatic feast to make a work of musical art that has enchanted men, women, and children for more than two hundred years.

He did this with spoken words (thus the designation of the opera as a singspiel), arias and duets, and other vocal combinations that move at a much greater pace than those in the typical Italian opera; grand choral moments that include stirring hymns; and orchestral instrument combinations that at times play off the opera's title but that also employ new kinds of musical diction for Mozart. Trombones (no less than three of them), for example, are a true part of this opera's orchestra, and the chimes that make the sound of Papageno's glockenspiel add a wonderful new coloristic element.

When all of these components come together in the glorious final scenes of *The Magic Flute,* when at last Tamino and Pamina sing, "Wir wandelten durch Feuergluten, Bekämpften mutig die Gefahr" (We have walked through flames, fought the danger bravely), and Tamino then plays his flute, we may all suspend belief and simply bask under a spell that no other composer has ever been able to conjure in quite this way, a musical potion that is itself magic.

TO PERUSE THE DISCOGRAPHY OF *The Magic Flute* is to conclude that practically every singer worth his or her salt has wanted to record this opera. There is even a 1975 movie version made by the great Swedish director Ingmar Bergman, with

MUSINGS ON

Beverly Sills on singing the Queen of the Night in *The Magic Flute*

Almost all of the Queen of the Night's part consists of two arias containing five high F's. I figured if I sang the role well, I'd impress the hell out of everybody—myself most of all.

That had to be the reason I did it, because I must tell you, the Queen of the Night is the most boring, pointless role I ever sang. The Queen of the Night sings an aria in Scene 1 of Act 1, and then sings another aria in Scene 3 of Act II. Between arias, you sit backstage for at least an hour and a half.

The one redeeming feature of the role is its difficulty. At any given time, only four or five sopranos in the world are able to sing the Queen of the Night. How high is a high F? Very high. In addition to those five high F's, the Queen's two arias contain some rather difficult coloratura passages. And you can't be a pipsqueak soprano, because the only bird the character resembles is a ravenous vulture. You've really got to be able to sock those notes out there, especially in the second act, when the Queen sings her vengeance aria. . . .

Because so few sopranos can sing the Queen of the Night, you can write your own ticket and live forever on that role. As soon as you perform it successfully a couple of times, you get an instant reputation. Every impresario puts you on his list, which is how you get to do Queen of the Night wherever you want. It's really astonishing—you can ask anything for singing the role, and you'll almost certainly get it. In the early days of my career, the highest fees I ever received were not for my Rosalindas, Violettas, and other roles, but for the Queen of the Night.

From *Beverly: An Autobiography* (1987)

a Swedish cast and an orchestra led by Eric Ericson (perhaps one of the inspirations for Joseph Losey's movie adaptation of *Don Giovanni* four years later). Other DVD versions include James Levine conducting the Vienna Philharmonic Orchestra and Bernhard Haitink with the London Philharmonic Orchestra; both of these productions offer excellent casts.

A personal favorite of many Mozarteans is Karl Böhm's beautiful 1966 Deutsche Grammophon (DG) recording with an extraordinary cast: Dietrich Fischer-Dieskau as Papageno, Lisa Otto as Papagena, Evelyn Lear as Pamina, Fritz Wunderlich as Tamino, Franz Crass as Sarastro, and Roberta Peters as the Queen of the Night. The orchestra in this rapturous account is the Berlin Philharmonic, with the RIAS-Kammerchor.

Other favorites include the great Sir Neville Marriner, once again with the Academy of St. Martin in the Fields, and Haitink again, this time with the Symphonierorchester des Bayerischen Rundfunks (Bavarian Radio Symphony Orchestra), in both cases with mostly lesser known but fine casts.

All-star singers join the indefatigable Sir Charles Mackerras, once again leading the Scottish Chamber Orchestra. Thomas Allen is Papageno, and the great Barbara Hendricks is Pamina. Fischer-Dieskau appears again on a fine old DG recording with the lesser-known Ferenc Fricsay leading the Berlin RIAS Choir and Symphony Orchestra, while Lucia Popp sings on Otto Klemperer's EMI recording, which also features the indomitable Elisabeth Schwarzkopf and Christa Ludwig. John Eliot Gardiner again leads the Monteverdi Choir and the English Baroque Orchestra in a DG recording.

Not to be overlooked is Mackerras and the London Philharmonic in a recorded performance of the opera with an English libretto. In this day and age of supertitles and other live translations of the original language of an opera, it is decidedly uncool in the view of many opera addicts to listen to a recording or attend a performance in which the language is not the original. Nevertheless, the music remains, and it is intriguing to see how the translator has coordinated his or her text with the nuances of the music.

Finally, many CDs include highlights of *The Magic Flute.* René Pape and Thomas Quasthoff are exemplary on the 2006 DG *Mozart Album.*

After the premier of *The Magic Flute*, Mozart plunged into his work on the Requiem, for which he had received the commission several months earlier. For a brief period, his efforts continued without respite, and he was joined at home by Constanze, who had returned from Baden, and their two children.

Nights found him at Schikaneder's theater, where *The Magic Flute* was now a major hit. Mozart went all the time, frequently taking along a friend. One night in October he even invited his old rival Salieri. Mozart happily reported afterward, "[He] liked not only my music but also the libretto and everything else. They [Salieri and his mistress] said it was a grand opera worthy of being performed at the grandest festivities and before the greatest monarch and that they'd certainly be seeing it more than once as they'd never seen a more beautiful or delightful spectacle. He listened and watched with the utmost attentiveness, and from the overture to the final chorus there wasn't a single number that didn't call forth a *bravo* or a *bello* from him."

Less than two months later, the writer of this letter, the composer of *The Magic Flute*, was dead.

CONCLUSION: MOZART AND MORTALITY

LIKE PARIS, THE CITY THAT HEMINGWAY ONCE CALLED "a moveable feast" in his memoir of the same name, Mozart and his music remain with you wherever you go, whatever you do. He is ubiquitous. His name has been given to something called the Mozart Effect, a trademarked term for the healing powers and the memory stimulus that Mozart's music is said by some to have. A surgeon at Harvard Medical School, who is also a musician, believes that Mozart "composed music the way he did partly because it made him feel better." Shop for classical CDs, and you will find more selections for Mozart than for any other composer. Decide to do some more reading, and you will discover enough books only on Mozart to fill a small library, with the prize perhaps going to the 2007 Yale University Press publication of Hermann Abert's monumental *W. A. Mozart,* lucidly translated by Stewart Spencer and brilliantly edited by Cliff Eisen—all 1,515 of its oversize pages with small type!

In a review of that book, itself a vastly expanded German edition of a nineteenth-century Mozart biography by Otto Jahn, the pianist and musicologist Charles Rosen furthered a debate about whether Mozart was, in his music, expressing himself, as Abert argues, or his listeners, as Eisen believes (and Rosen assents with qualifications). "Mozart was a keen observer of mankind, and boundlessly empathetic," according to Eisen, "but what he expressed in his music was us, not himself." Well, who's to say? As Eisen himself goes on to admit, "At the most basic level . . . I agree, not only that Mozart's music is profoundly expressive but also as to what it expresses."

Several years ago, a British writer named Alain de Botton published a book called *How Proust Can Change Your Life.* Moving back and forth between quotations from Proust's magnum opus, *Remembrance of Things Past,* and his own experience, de Botton not only creates an entertaining way to approach Proust but also extracts maxims from his work that turn the great French author into a kind of self-help guru. It is no stretch to imagine Mozart's music having the same power, his music serving as the inspiration for a volume entitled *Mozart's Guide to Life.*

Consider Mahler, the great anti-Mozart example in both form and execution. Few musical experiences are more thrilling than hearing a great performance of one of his choral symphonies. We can say the same of Beethoven's Ninth or Benjamin Britten's *War Requiem.*

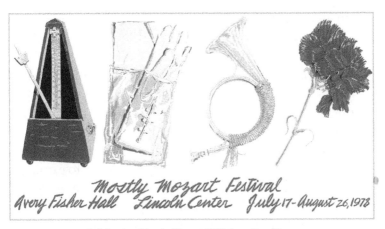

Mostly Mozart Festival
Avery Fisher Hall Lincoln Center July 17–August 26, 1978

Celebrating Mostly Mozart 1978, from Don Nice.

But who would ever put on a recording of these works to start his or her day? And one cannot imagine them as the music for a wedding or a funeral.

You might, on the other hand, listen to Mozart's Symphony no. 39 in any place, at any time, and under any circumstance. And you could say this about several other Mozart symphonies, most of his piano concertos, and large portions of the da Ponte operas. In fact, many people already *do* listen to his music with that sort of frequency; it is part of the fabric of their lives. They even "play" favorites, hearing the first movement of the twenty-fifth piano concerto in their heads, for example, as they go about their workday.

It is no accident that every day between noon and one in the afternoon, a New England NPR station plays at least one Mozart piece. Nor is it a coincidence that Mozart's music has inspired the concept of an "effect." And can it be a surprise that the list of Proust's favorite composers did not include Mozart? Mozart is the supreme anti-nostalgist, an apparent paradox since the extraordinary beauty of his music is a paradigm of the kind of lyricism we often associate with nostalgia.

"A sentimentalist," F. Scott Fitzgerald, the author of *The Great Gatsby*, once wrote, "believes things will last forever, whereas a romantic has a desperate confidence they will not."

By that definition, Mozart was a romantic—another paradox, since the art he created may be as close to earning the sobriquet *eternal* as anything since the Parthenon.

In the great works of Mahler, Wagner, Beethoven and other mostly nineteenth-century giants, there is always at least one moment of apotheosis; the music builds toward this moment and calms down after the moment has passed.

In Mozart, on the other hand, these moments occur and reoccur with a dramatic and aesthetic regularity that is at complete odds with the idea of apotheosis. For Mozart, *every* moment is as precious as life itself, every breath, every note, every beat, every phrase. With regard to Mozart, not only the concept or quality of nostalgia but also the very significance of human memory takes on a wholly different meaning, which is the key, the source, of his singular power to soothe, heal, inspire, move, contain, grasp, affirm, assuage, develop, conjure, make one . . . it's a long list, and the direct objects of these verbs have been left out because they form an even longer litany.

Recall how, in the extended finale of *The Marriage of Figaro*'s second act, an argument has been taking place over the authorship of a mysterious letter that the Count has discovered. In a hilarious exchange, Figaro must deny any involvement. He pleads for a happy ending, at which point he is joined first by Susanna and later by the Countess.

The dramatic climax of the sequence is conveyed musically with the introduction of a ground bass—a single sustained note underneath all of the others, played by the horn, that strongly serves to remind us of the supreme importance of every moment, how even at the most ridiculous of times our feelings can be at their most exposed and vulnerable.

It is all over in a few minutes, even this scene in the opera rapidly moving on to something else, but there will be another surprise for us there. We can count on it, count on Mozart in the music to teach us something else—no, not to teach, but to share. Never dogmatic, Mozart comes across finally as a fellow traveler—not a guide, really, but a companion. Mozart's music becomes, then, the best company a person could ever have. It is a blessing like the ascendance of the melody line in the Laudate Dominum from the Vespers, K. 339. How natural it seems, like breathing: we breathe with it and in so doing we, too, make a kind of ascent.

Listen again to that glorious, repeated figure in the second movement of the *Jupiter* Symphony, when Mozart employs the Baroque rhythmic figure called a hemiola. The tension that is released in the music becomes a release in our lives: we let it go, just as the music does.

Mozart's remarkable use of hemiolas creates the impression that the movement is in 2/4 time (two beats to a measure with a quarter note getting a beat), but it is actually in 3/4 time (three beats to a measure, with a quarter note still getting one beat). The hemiola technique occurs throughout the 101-measure movement, first appearing in the 23rd measure. In many of these instances, the bass line moves in a pattern of four eighth notes (two of which equal one quarter note), suggesting 2/4 time. It is not the grouping of six eighth notes we would expect in 3/4 time.

By what artistic logic did Mozart do this? We might just as well ask why it is Mozart's music that has survived the ages. Why do we listen to Mozart and not to his contemporaries who were important at the time but are now long forgotten? One reason is that Mozart found ways to take a shared form of communication, in this case the classical sonata allegro form, and to transform it from a generic formula into a highly varied yet intensely specific musical story. Voilà, the *Jupiter* hemiolas.

In simplest terms, the classical sonata allegro form is an organizing principle for single movements of several different kinds of musical compositions, including the symphony. The basic format begins with the exposition, in which one or more themes are set out; followed by the development, in which the composer plays with or varies the theme(s) from the exposition; before the movement concludes with the recapitulation, the meaning of which is self-evident. Thus, the form encompasses a kind of musical narrative or story.

The "story" of the *Jupiter* Symphony's second movement begins with the introduction of the first hemiola. The tension created by the hemiola doesn't seem to fit the rather placid character of the movement's opening. Something has happened, something disturbing. According to the rules of classical musical engagement, the rest of the piece must therefore respond, within the sonata allegro form, to this "disturbance." Mozart achieves this response—this satisfying working out of the compositional and emotional proportioning or the resolution of this disturbance, its reversibility—in several ways.

The brief development—only one-third the length of both the exposition and the recapitulation, which are similar in length—deals directly with the disturbance alone.

Mozart understands that the shock of measure 19 must bedealt with immediately; it cannot wait for the recapitulation. If he had waited until the recapitulation, he would have had to extend its length in order to reduce the impact of the music's eventual return to the placid character of the opening.

Instead of repeating the opening as if nothing has happened, the recapitulation begins with a varied restatement of the movement's first eleven measures. Not until much later does Mozart introduce marchlike music, which has not been heard before. Why has he done this? To distract us from the expected, the missing recapitulation of measure 19—the music, its argument or disturbance, that he must reverse. And one of the ways he does this is through the use of hemiolas. Several moments in the recapitulation sound like six measures in the meter of 2/4, rather than what they actually are, four measures of 3/4. A distraction, in other words, has been made through the repetition of a rhythmic device that has appeared numerous times before, a beautiful example of a formula made distinctive through its saturation in the piece.

When measure 19 finally does appear later in the recapitulation, it's not literally transposed, again as one would expect, but instead remembered in a ghostly variation. Mozart acknowledges its presence not as a formulaic repetition but as a musical recollection of something once important but now reduced in impact.

The end of the movement, at least in terms of the literal recapitulation of these measures, doesn't occur when we think it should. Instead, the music continues with yet another statement of the very first measure in the movement. Again, why does Mozart do this? Because he realizes that while measure 19 has finally been forgotten, he still hasn't established a kind of musical equilibrium that will make all of this fit together, a music that will unify the varying pulsations of the movement.

In the first four of the movement's final seven measures, Mozart gives us the only music in the entire movement that repeats itself in the same key with both the same register and the same instrumentation. This is the music that allows both the placid and the disturbing music to coexist. As an example of sonata allegro form, the *Jupiter* Symphony is very unconventional. But it is exactly this individuality that distinguishes Mozart from every composer who lived from 1760 to 1820, with the exceptions of Haydn and Beethoven. We understand that his novel use of the form is a creative way of presenting a sequence of events, a "story," that communicates an emotion. Centuries later, this unique approach is why Mozart's music still moves us and sounds fresh.

Can it be an accident that in 2008 the great pianist Alfred Brendel, in his last public performance before retiring from the concert stage, chose Mozart's Piano Concerto no. 9, K. 271, from the hundreds of works in his repertoire? Mozart was only twenty-one years old when he wrote this piece, aptly nicknamed *Jeune homme* (Young Man), but to hear it you might imagine that the composer had lived a long life and was in this music reflecting on and marshaling the accumulated wisdom of many years.

And you might, as you listened, reflect on your own passage through life, from buoyant optimism to sanguine stoicism to enraptured celebration to melancholy tenderness. You might pause if you could—not at a concert, of course, but certainly while listening to a recording—at a point midway in the second movement, just a throwaway, to judge by Mozart standards, barely lasting more than a few seconds, when the piano, breaking away from the main theme, springs into the most gorgeous series of mini arpeggios, one upon another yearning, as it were, to remain high on the keyboard as, alas, they descend in a cascade of sound that is almost unbearably beautiful.

Almost. It is the great Mozart word, the word that brings us to listen and then gets us to listen again, no different, if you think about it, than that promise we all make to ourselves now and then as we wake up or embrace someone we love or say good-bye, as in, "I think I've got it now, I think . . . I hope . . . I feel . . . as if things will be okay, I really do, because, well . . . I mean, what he said . . . what she did . . . I really do think I understand it now . . . almost."

Imagining the arc of that impulse, we may find ourselves searching in the music for clues to the mysterious essence of our shared being. Mozart, we reflect, saw the same sun rise, heard a similar rustling of the wind, felt this identical loss of a friendship or love. We may even at such moments—that Mozart word again—find ourselves conjuring, as we strain to comprehend what our hearts can feel but no document records. Listening, we dream, and in that reverie are buoyed by a renewed conviction in the triumphant goodness of art.

Play it again, Amadé.

A PERSONAL NOTE

On a recent autumn afternoon, I ran into an acquaintance, a retired air force colonel who was once a fighter pilot in Vietnam and later flew cargo planes in the Persian Gulf War. During a conversation centered on catching up about kids, the election, and the sorry state of our respective golf games, the subject of music came up. My friend told me that when he's in his car driving a long distance, or even when he's just feeling stressed, he listens to Mozart.

It's a confession I've heard from others. I've never once said "Mozart" to someone and not gotten back a response. People invariably have something to contribute to the conversation, even if they are not musicians. It's a striking phenomenon, unlikely to be triggered by mentioning any other composer, or even an exotic locale or recent movie.

"What is it in this music that draws him, draws all of us?" I asked myself afterward, about my air force friend.

"What is the source of the music's power?" And I kept surmising that this question about Mozart is not a summation but a jumping-off point, indeed the very thread of the entire fabric.

A few months later, another encounter with a friend, this one planned, prompted the same conclusion. It was late winter and I was on my way to Boston to hear James Levine, one of the great Mozart interpreters of our time, conduct a rehearsal of the Boston Symphony Orchestra (BSO). Maestro Levine, music director of both the BSO and the Metropolitan Opera, was preparing the orchestra for a performance of Mozart's last three symphonies, a program that I had heard them present less than two years before during a summer concert at Tanglewood under guest conductor Kurt Masur. For Masur, the former music director of the New York Philharmonic, that concert had been a repeat of his very first BSO program more than twenty-five years earlier, as well as a commemoration of his eightieth birthday. I remembered that concert well, how beautifully the orchestra had played and with what economy of motion Masur had conducted, often raising both barely moving arms before him with wrists slightly bent, palms facing the floor, as if in a blessing. What would Levine—Jimmy, to everyone around him—add to or change in the interpretation?

Accompanying me on my field trip—a two-hour drive from my home—was a fifty-five-year-old business-man who'd sold his equipment and parts factory and taken early retirement. For a brief time he'd been the cofounder and impresario of a popular café, but now the main focus of his ambition was a sailboat he'd bought the year before, which was now awaiting the spring in nearby Newport, Rhode Island. Though he had grown up and lived his entire life in Massachusetts, and is the father of two sons who are both musicians, he had never been to a concert at Boston's Symphony Hall.

We arrived so early that we had time for coffee across the street, before making our way to the brick temple of music the BSO has called home for more than a century. In the lobby, I learned our passes were at the stage door, from which we followed the labyrinthine hallways to the actual auditorium. We walked upstairs another flight and found seats in the first row of the first balcony, stage right and near the sidewall, where we could not only eavesdrop on the orchestra's members as they warmed up but also, once the rehearsal began, be able to hear what the maestro would have to say to them about Mozart.

Casually dressed in slacks and a long-sleeved pullover, his bushy, curly hair forming a kind of wild penumbra above his large, wrinkled brow and piercing eyes, Levine ambled onstage, greeting several of the instrumentalists by name. Finally he stepped up onto the podium. Looking first at the rehearsal clock, he turned now to those in the auditorium, some of whom had no doubt come to this open rehearsal thinking, as I had, that what we were going to hear would be pretty close to a concert performance, with few breaks and fewer words. We would soon learn how wrong our prediction had been, as Levine patiently and passionately worked, in some cases measure by measure, on parts of each piece, meticulously shaping what I was certain would be a grand performance that night.

But first, taking a microphone in one hand, Levine wanted to say good morning and to explain that we had to wait another two minutes to begin, the unstated reason being the strict rules that govern the orchestra's labor contract. He seemed amused by this requirement and took the opportunity to announce that the order of music would be scrambled—my word, not his—with the fortieth, or G-minor, symphony first, followed by the forty-first, or *Jupiter*, and then finally the thirty-ninth, which he simply referred to as the E-flat. And then he added a little grace note to these remarks, which was that all this music was as great—his word—as anything anyone had ever written. By then it was 10:30 A.M., and he took his place in his chair on the podium, and, looking around now at his orchestra, he waited another moment, smiling, and at last, with a graceful upraising of his arms, began.

Watching and listening to all of this, I had briefly forgotten my friend, with whom I had been engaged in prerehearsal conversation about the music, of course, but also about the stock market; he had been trying to explain to me what a hedge fund was. We'd talked a little about families, too, especially his, which would soon be gathering for a reunion in California. He was not sure how to convey the deep emotions the event represented to him. But from the very first notes of the symphony, it was clear that Mozart had understood them when he composed this magnificence during just a few short weeks of that mysterious summer of 1788.

Yes, I thought, as it all came back to me in these first notes—the seemingly simple figure, little more than an elaborated appoggiatura, the violins singing and then soaring ever so tenuously. And next to me, as if by some celestial cue, I sensed in the sighs of my friend's rhythmic breathing a shared consciousness in the clarity and purity, the brevity and eternity, of this Mozart moment.

READING MOZART

With the wonderful exception of the Mozart family letters, all of the voluminous material about Mozart comes from secondary sources. But what sources! You could read a thousand words a day about the composer for an entire year, and hardly have scratched the surface of what is available just in English.

That said, you might keep certain priorities in mind when you create your Mozart library. An excellent place to begin is Peter Gay's short biography *Mozart* (New York: Penguin, 1999), a lively, opinionated narrative driven by a thematic analysis of Mozart's development. An even shorter but comprehensive and authoritative account is the late Mozart scholar Stanley Sadie's Mozart entry in *The New Grove Dictionary of Music and Musicians* (New York: Oxford University Press, 2001), which is also available online and in a paperback edition. Among Sadie's other works is *Mozart: The Early Years* (New York: W.W. Norton & Co., 2006), which is notable for Sadie's masterly synthesis of music and biography.

No single Mozart book, however, is more magisterial in command of its subject (and more mammoth in size) than Hermann Abert's *W. A. Mozart,* beautifully translated by Stewart Spencer and lovingly edited by Cliff Eisen (New Haven: Yale University Press, 2008). This extraordinary book, first published in German in the early 1920s as a vast expansion of a nineteenth-century study by Otto Jahn, includes an enormous amount of technical, musical analysis, all handled within Abert's perceptive analysis of Mozart's life. Bonus features include a complete catalog of Mozart's works and an appendix of the so-called Bäsle letters, which Mozart wrote to his cousin Maria Anna Thekla.

The same team of Spencer and Eisen has also produced *Wolfgang Amadeus Mozart: A Life in Letters* (New York: Penguin, 2006), a splendid new translation of Mozart letters along with detailed, informative notes. Emily Anderson's earlier translation of the letters has been revised and updated by Stanley Sadie and Fiona Smart (New York: W. W. Norton & Co., 1985).

Among recent popular treatments, Jane Glover's *Mozart's Women: His Family, His Friends, His Music* (New York: HarperCollins, 2005) incorporates compulsively readable sections about the composer's operas into portraits that include Mozart's wife, Constanze, one of the many sopranos in the composer's life. David Cairns's *Mozart and His Operas* (Berkeley: University of California Press, 2006) is an extended love letter to Mozart's operas such is the author's passion for the music. For the serious student, this subject is explored further in Andrew Steptoe's *The Mozart–Da Ponte Operas: The Cultural and Musical Background to Le nozze di Figaro, Don Giovanni, and Così fan Tutte* (New York: Oxford University Press, 1990).

Piero Melograni's *Wolfgang Amadeus Mozart: A Biography,* translated into English by Lydia G. Cochrane (Chicago: University of Chicago Press, 2007), presents a spirited narrative of Mozart's life without getting bogged down in the documentation of everything Mozart composed. Eric Bloom's much earlier *Mozart* (London: Dent, 1974), on the other hand, organizes its chronology around the works themselves, neatly highlighting and summarizing them. An affectionately eclectic approach propels *Amadeus: A Mozart Mosaic* by Herbert Kupferberg (New York: McGraw-Hill, 1986).

For many Mozartians, Maynard Solomon's *Mozart: A Life* (New York: HarperCollins, 1995) remains the definitive, modern source, though not everyone will agree with the author's psychological analysis of the composer, particularly about the nature of his relationship with his father, Leopold.

Perhaps no contemporary writer has written and published more words about Mozart than the musicologist H. C. Robbins Landon. His many fascinating and informative books include *1791: Mozart's Last Year* (New York: Thames and Hudson, 1999), *Mozart: The Golden Years* (New York: Thames and Hudson, 2006), and a volume he edited called *The Mozart Essays* (New York: Thames and Hudson, 1995). Also of note is his *Mozart and Vienna* (New York: G. Schirmer, 1991). Among other collections of essays, an excellent choice is *The Compleat Mozart: A Guide to the Musical Works* by Neal Zaslaw with William Cowdery (New York: W. W. Norton & Co., 1990).

Because of Mozart's ubiquity, the pleasure of browsing often yields gratifying discoveries. Many of Michael Steinberg's fine program notes, most of them originally written for the Boston Symphony Orchestra, the San

Francisco Symphony, and the New York Philharmonic, have been collected in *The Symphony: A Listener's Guide* (New York: Oxford University Press, 1995); the volume includes six terrific essays about Mozart's final six symphonies.

Published material about Mozart in magazines, newspapers, online sites, and liner notes is beyond calibration. A good starting point is the Mozart Project, http://www.mozartproject.org/.

1. Joseph Solman, ed., *Mozartiana* (New York: Walker & Company, 1990), p. 27.
2. "Report on Survey to Determine the Feasibility of Creating and Operating a Performing Arts Center in New York City," Day & Zimmerman, Engineers, 1955, LCPA
3. Schuyler Chapin Oral History, 1991
4. Lincoln Center Executive Committee Minutes, September 9, 1963
5. Raymond Ericson, "Music: Mozart Series Is Off to an Excellent Start," *The New York Times,* August 2, 1966
6. Allan Kozinn, "Has Mostly Mozart Festival Worn Out Its Welcome?", *The New York Times,* August 27, 1992
7. "Basically Bill & Frankly Frederick," *Stagebill,* 1991
8. Gerard Schwarz Oral History, 2001
9. Ibid.
10. Ibid.
11. Ibid.
12. Allan Kozinn, "A Finale, Entirely, for Mozart and Schwarz," *The New York Times,* August 27, 2001

13. Martha Hostetter, "The Mostly Mozart Strike: Music, Money and Maybe Better Art," *Gotham Gazette,* September 1, 2002

14. Peter G. Davis, "Moz Def," *www.newyorkmetro.com,* 2003

15. "Avery Fisher Hall Reconfigured for Mostly Mozart Festival, Summer 2005," Lincoln Center, Inc. , press Release, May 3, 2005, LCPA.

CREDITS

Illustrations on pages ii, 11, 13, 15, 18, 22, 24, 41, 44, 57, 74, 97, 136, 163, 170, 194 courtesy of the New York Public Library; photos on pages x, 142, 155, 203 by James Dee; photos on pages 3, 54, 67, 83, 99, 118, 119 by Susanne Faulkner Stevens; page 76 courtesy of Sir James Galway; page 102 courtesy of the Lincoln Center archive.

INDEX

Abbado, Claudio, 54, *54*
Abduction from the Seraglio,
  The. *See Entführung aus dem
  Serail, Die* (The Abduction
  from the Seraglio)
Abert, Hermann, 202
Abraham, F. Murray, 14
Academy of St. Martin in the
  Fields, 53, 100, 122, 197
Adagio in E, K. 261, 75
Allen, Thomas, 197
Allen Berg Quartett, 82
Amadeus (film), 8, 14
Amadeus (play), 8
Anderson, Emily, 21, 23
Auden, W. H., 178–179
Auger, Arleen, 99
Ave verum corpus, K. 618, 95,
  96–97, 101
Ax, Emanuel, 83, 130–131

Bach, C. P. E., 68
Bach, Johann Sebastian, 32, 51,
  61, 112, 126
  influence on Mozart, 81, 93
  Mass in B Minor, 89
  Saint Matthew Passion, 89

Bach, P. D. Q. (Peter
  Schickele), 51
Bach Collegium, 99
Baechler, Donald, 155
Barenboim, Daniel, 53, 119,
  119, 192–193
basso clarinets, 75
Bastien und Bastienne, 140
Bavarian Radio Chorus and
  Orchestra, 99, 197
Beaumarchais, Pierre, 165
Beethoven, Ludwig van, 32, 34,
  39, 46, 134
Bergman, Ingmar, 195–196
Berlin Philharmonic Orchestra,
  53, 99, 186, 197
Berlin RIAS Choir and Sym-
  phony Orchestra, 197
Berlioz, Hector, 95, 121,
  158–159, 184–185
Bernstein, Leonard, 54, 99
Berry, Walter, 167
Beyer, Franz, 98
Bilson, Malcolm, 121
Böhm, Karl, 167, 186, 192, 197
Borge, Victor, 20
Brain, Dennis, 75

Brendel, Alfred, 119, 122, 124–125, 128–129, 208
Brilliant, 54
Brüggen, Frans, 53
Budapest String Quartet, 82
Burgtheater (Vienna), 24, 162
Bush, Jack, *102*
Busoni, Ferruccio, 125, 129

cadenzas
   about, 113–114
   cadenza, K. 624, 114
Callas, Maria, 95
Celebrating Mostly Mozart, 1978 (Nice), *203*
chamber music
   Haydn Quartets, K. 387, 421, 428, 458, 464, 465, 79–80, 82–84
   for piano, 125–126
   Piano Quartets nos. 1 and 2, K. 478 and K. 493, 83, 86
   recordings of, 82–83
   String Quartet in B-flat, K. 465 *(The Hunt),* 84
   String Quartet in E-flat, K. 428, 81–82
   String Quintets, K. 174, 406, 515, 516, 593, 614, 79–80, 84–85
   "subject" of, 81–82
Chopin, Frédéric, 31, 73
choral music. *See* vocal music
chronology, of Mozart's life, 26–27
Ciofi, Patrizia, 167
Clarinet Concerto in A Major, K. 622, 71, 75, 77, 97

Clemency of Titus, The. *See clemenza di Tito, La,* K. 621 (The Clemency of Titus)
Clementi, Muzio, 110
clemenza di Tito, la, K. 621 (The Clemency of Titus), 92, 96, 105, 188–189
Colloredo, Count Hieronymus von (archbishop of Salzburg), 15–16, 89, 147–150
concertante, 63–67
   Concertone, K. 186, 66, 67
   Concertone, K. 190, 37, 67–69
   Eine kleine Nachtmusik (A Little Night Music), K. 525, 66, 67, 69–70
   Gran Partita, Serenade in B-flat, K. 361, 66–69
   recordings of, 66–67
   Sinfonia Concertante, K. 364, 66, 69–70, 75
concert arias, 153–154
Concerto Köln, 167
Concertone, K. 186, 66, 67
Concertone, K. 190, 37, 67–69
concertos, 71–75
   Clarinet Concerto in A Major, K. 622, 71, 75, 77, 97
   Concerto no. 14, K. 449, 131
   Concerto no. 23 in A Major, K. 488, 133–134
   Concerto no. 27 in B-flat Major, K. 595, 114–115, 135
   Concerto no. 24 in C Minor, K. 491, 134

Concerto no. 26 in D Major, K. 537, 135

Concerto no. 20 in D Minor, K. 466, 109, 113, 123, 130–132

Concerto no. 22 in E-flat Major, K. 482, 133

Coronation Concerto, K. 537, 114–115, 135

Flute Concertos nos. 1 and 2, K. 313 and K. 314, 77–78

Horn Concertos nos. 1 through 4, K. 412/514, 417, 447, 495, 77–78

for multiple pianos, 125–126

recordings of, 75–76, 117–123

Violin Concertos nos. 1 through 5, K. 207, 211, 216, 218, 219, 76–77

See also piano concertos; piano music

Conegliano, Emanuele. *See* da Ponte, Lorenzo

Copland, Aaron, 156–157

copyists, 64–65

Coronation Concerto, K. 537, 114–115, 135

Coronation Mass, K. 317, 89, 92

Così fan tutte (Women Are Like That), 104–105, 143, 180–187

love theme of, 161

story of, 180–185

counterpoint, 81

Crass, Franz, 197

dances, 137

da Ponte, Lorenzo, 104–105, 133, 154–159, 170–171, 173–174, 190

Davis, Sir Colin, 75

de Botton, Alain, 202

Decca, 168, 180

de Larrocha, Alicia, *118,* 119

de Peyer, Gervase, 75

Deutsche Grammophon, 43, 53, 66, 99, 167–168, 180, 186, 197

DG Archiv, 121, 152–153, 186, 197, 198

Divertimento in E-flat Major, K. 563, 83

divertimentos, 66

Domingo, Placido, 144, 151

Don Giovanni, 168–180, *170*

Ax on, 130–131

commission for, 21, 124, 166

Copland on, 158–159

Levine on, 104–105

love as theme of, 161

popularity of, 68, 194–195

Prague premiere of, 36, 178

story of, 91, 140, 143, 173–179

Don Giovanni (film), 197

Edinburgh Festival Choir and Orchestra, 187

Eine kleine Nachtmusik (A Little Night Music), K. 525, 66, 67, 69–70

Ein musikalischer Spass (A Musical Joke), K. 522, 68

Einstein, Alfred, 40–42

Eisen, Cliff, 202
EMI, 43, 100, 153, 180, 186, 197
English Baroque Orchestra, 180, 186, 197
English Baroque Soloists, 121, 152
English Chamber Orchestra, 32, 53, 122
Entführung aus dem Serail, Die (The Abduction from the Seraglio), 58, 105, 145, 150, 152–153, 157
epistle sonatas, 101
Epstein, Steve, 83
Ericson, Eric, 197
Exsultate jubilate in F Major, K. 165, 37, 94, 100
Eybler, Joseph, 98

fantasies
about, 109, 137
Fantasia in C Minor, K. 475, 137
finta semplice, La (The Pretended Simpleton), 140
first cantata, K. 42, 102
Fischer-Dieskau, Dietrich, 132, 168, 197
Fitzgerald, F. Scott, 204
Fleming, Renée, 186, 191
Flute Concertos nos. 1 and 2, K. 313 and K. 314, 77–78
Forman, Milos, 8
fortepiano, 10, 110
Freiberg Baroque Orchestra, 55
Fricsay, Ferenc, 197
Fugue in C Minor, K. 426, 138
Furtwängler, Wilhelm, 67, 180

Gachinger Kantorei, 99
Galway, Sir James, 75, 76, 78
Gardiner, John Eliot, 99, 121, 152–153, 180, 186, 197
Gay, Peter, 25
German Dances, 66
German Opera and Chorus, 168
Gilfry, Rodney, 180
Giulini, Carlo Maria, 180
Goode, Richard, 80
Gottlieb, Amadé, 9. *See also* Mozart, Johannes Chrysostomus Wolfgangus Theophilus Amadeus (Wolfgang Amadeus)
Gould, Glenn, 126
Gran Partita, Serenade in B-flat, K. 361, 66–69
Great Performers series (Lincoln Center), 54, 83, 118
Grumiaux, Arthur, 75
Grumiaux Quartett, 82

Haffner, Sigmund, 45–46
Haffner Symphony, no. 35, K. 385, 45–46, 57–58
Haitink, Bernhard, 197
Hampson, Thomas, 180, 186
Harding, Daniel, 180
Harmonia Mundi, 167
Harnoncourt, Nikolaus, 145
Haydn, Franz Joseph, 32, 34, 39, 47, 73, 188
chamber music dedicated to, 79–80, 82–84, 109
influence on Mozart, 81
Haydn, Michael, 47, 123

Haydn Quartets, K. 387, 421,
    428, 458, 464, 465, 79–80,
    82–84, 109
Heifetz, Jascha, 74
hemiolas, 50, 205–207
Hendricks, Barbara, 100, 197
Hogwood, Christopher, 99, *99*
Horn Concertos nos. 1 through
    4, K. 412/514, 417, 447,
    495, 77–78
*How Proust Can Change Your
    Life* (de Botton), 202
Hulce, Tom, 14
Hunt, The. See String Quartet in
    B-flat, K. 465 *(The Hunt)*

Idomeneo, 145, 146–154
Israel Philharmonic Orchestra, 67
iTunes, 54

Jacobs, René, 55, 167
Jahn, Otto, 46, 202
Janzer, Georges, 82
Joseph II, Emperor, 188
Juan, Don, 169
Jupiter Symphony, no. 41,
    K. 551, 37–38, 49–50, 53,
    61–62, 205–208

Kallman, Chester, 178–179
Kanawa, Kiri Te, 168, 186
Kapilow, Rob, 32–33
Keats, John, 168
Kelly, Michael, 162–164
Kempff, Wilhelm, 132
Kleiber, Erich, 168
Klemperer, Otto, 197
Köchel, Ludwig von, 35

Krips, Josef, 32, 179–180
Kundera, Milan, 32–33
Kyrie in D Minor, K. 341, 100

Laredo, Jaime, 83
Lear, Evelyn, 197
Le Gros, Jean, 56
Leopold II, Emperor,
    92, 135, 190
Leppard, Raymond, 75
Levine, James, 104–105, 186, 197
Levy, Amnon, 72
libretto. *See* da Ponte, Lorenzo
Lieberson, Lorraine Hunt, 153
Lied von der Erde, Das (The
    Song of the Earth)
    (Mahler), 52
Lincoln Center (New York
    City)
    Great Performers series, *54,
        83, 118*
    Mostly Mozart Festival, 1–3,
        3, 67, 102, 142, 155, 203
Linz Symphony, no. 36, K. 425,
    47–48, 58–59, 93
London Philharmonic
    Orchestra, 197, 198
London Philharmonic
    Orchestra and Chorus,
    168, 187
London Symphony Orchestra,
    54, 75
Lorengar, Pilar, 187
Losey, Joseph, 197
love themes
    of *The Magic Flute,* 161, 190
    of Mozart/da Ponte collabo-
        rations, 161, 182

Ludwig, Christa, 187, 197
Lupu, Radu, 125

Ma, Yo-Yo, 83, *83*
Mackerras, Sir Charles, 32, 153,
  167, 187, 197–198
Magic Flute, The, 105,
  187–199, *194*
  love theme of, 161, 190
  popularity of, 139
  story of, 90–91, 190–195
  technique and, 143, 146
  Vienna premiere of, 96–97
Magic Flute, The (film), 195–196
Mahler, Gustav, 31, 52, 56, 95,
  120, 202–203
Marlboro Music Festival
  (Vermont), 80
Marriage of Figaro, The, 21,
  88, 116–117, 133–134,
  160–168, *163*
  love as theme of, 161, 182
  popularity of, 48, 59, 64,
  104–105
  story of, 143, 204–205
  Vienna premiere of, 124,
  162–164
Marriner, Sir Neville, 53, 100,
  122, 197
Marsalis, Wynton, 48
Masonic Cantata, K. 623, 97,
  101–102
Masonic Funeral Music,
  K. 477, 97
Masons, 13, 90–91
masses, 89–91
  Coronation Mass,
  K. 317, 89, 92

Mass in B Minor (Bach), 89
Mass in C Minor, K. 427,
  90–91, 92–93, 100
Requiem Mass in
  D Minor, K. 626, 33, 35,
  88, 90, 96–100, 103, 198
Maunder, Richard, 98
Mehta, Zubin, 66–67
Memoirs (Berlioz), 121, 184–185
Metropolitan Opera
  (New York), 194
Milnes, Sherrill, 174–175
minuets, 66, 137
Monteverdi Choir, 197
Mostly Mozart Festival
  (Lincoln Center), 1–3, *3,*
  67, 102, 142, *155, 203*
Motherwell, Robert, *3*
Moyse, Marcel, 80
Mozart, Canada (town), 16
Mozart, Constanze Weber
  (wife), 17, *18,* 48
  children of, 10, 36, 49, 93,
  106–107, 188
  copyists supervised by, 65
  courtship of, 10, 17, 20, 48,
  90–91, 150
  health of, 36, 188
  Leopold Mozart and, 90–91
  Requiem and, 88, 97–98
  as singer, 93–94
Mozart, Johannes Chrysostomus
  Wolfgangus Theophilus
  Amadeus (Wolfgang
  Amadeus), 7–9, *41,*
  97, 136
  childhood of, 10–13, *11, 13,*
  139–141

children of, 10, 36, 49, 93, 106–107, 188

chronology, 26–27

Colloredo and, 15–16, 89, 147–150

composing style of, 19, 39, 52–53, 64–65

da Ponte collaboration, 104–105, 133, 154–159, 170–171, 173–174, 190

death of, 25–26

father's influence on, 17–26, 39, 53, 58, 115 (*See also* Mozart, Leopold (father))

as *Konzertmeister* (Salzburg), 15

legacy of, 201–209

marriage of, 10, 17, 20, 48, 90–91, 150 (*See also* Mozart, Constanze Weber (wife))

on "melancholy," 160

music catalogued by Köchel numbers, 35

orchestration by, 50, 52, 71–75, 162, 205–207

as performer, 10, 71–75, *74*, 94–95, 106–107, 124

politics and, 90–91

in Salzburg, 14–17, *15*

students of, 88

in Vienna, 17–26, *24*

volume of work, 31–35, 52–53

See also individual musical genres; individual names of compositions

Mozart, Leopold (father), 7, 10–12, *11*, 17–26, 39, *44*

composing by, 15, 43–44

correspondence with son, 21, 23, 53, 58, 115, 147–150

on son's composing, 47, 123–124

on son's operas, 140

on son's romances, 17, 90–91

as son's teacher, 88

on son's violin playing, 73

Mozart, Maria Anna (mother), 17, 44–45, 56–57, *57*

Mozart, Maria Anna "Nannerl" (sister), 10–12, *11,* 49, 123, 137

Mozart, Maria Anna Thekla "Bäsle" (cousin), 22, *22*

Mozart, Theresia (daughter), 36, 49

Mozart Album, 198

Mozart and Salieri (Pushkin), 14, 106

Mozart Effect, 201

Mozart House (Salzburg), *15*

Mozart House (Vienna), 25

My Favorite Intermissions (Borge, Sherman), 20

Naxos, 67, 75

NDR Symphony Orchestra, 53

"negative capability," 168

Newman, Ernest, 185

New Philharmonia Orchestra, 75

Nice, Don, *203*

Nicolai Church (Vienna), 25–26

Niemetschek, Franz, 162

Norrington, Roger, 99

Olson, Stanford, 152
opera, 104–105, 139–146
  Bastien und Bastienne, 140
  concert arias and, 153–154
  Così fan tutte (Women Are
    Like That), 104–105, 143,
    161, 180–187
  da Ponte collaboration
    with Mozart, 104–105,
    133, 154–159, 170–171,
    173–174, 190
  Die Entführung aus dem Serail
    (The Abduction from the
    Seraglio), 58, 105, 145,
    150, 152–153, 157
  Don Giovanni, 21, 36, 68, 91,
    104–105, 124, 130–131,
    140, 143, 158–159, 161,
    168–180, *170,* 194–195
  Idomeneo, 145, 146–154
  Il re pastore, K. 208, 145
  Italian singers/productions,
    141, 158 (*See also*
    individual names of
    opera singers)
  La clemenza di Tito, K. 621
    (The Clemency of Titus),
    92, 96, 105, 188–189
  La finta semplice, 140
  The Magic Flute, 90–91,
    96–97, 105, 139, 143, 146,
    187–199, *194*
  The Marriage of Figaro, 21,
    48, 59, 64, 88, 104–105,
    116–117, 124, 133–134,
    143, 158, 160–168, *163,*
    204–205
  as Mozart's favorite genre, 13
  operatic terms, defined,
    145–146
  recordings of, 152–153,
    167–168, 179–180,
    186–187, 195–197
  Zaide, K. 344, 145
  See also vocal music
opera buffa, 145, 165
opera seria, 145
Orchestra Mozart, 54
Orchestra of the Age of
  Enlightenment, 186, 187
Orchestra of the Eighteenth
  Century, 53–54
orchestration, 71–75, 162
  basso clarinets, 75
  hemiolas, 50, 205–207
  woodwinds, 52
  See also individual genres of
    music; individual titles
    of works
organ, 110
Orgonasova, Luba, 152
Orpheus Chamber
  Orchestra, 66
Otto, Lisa, 197

Pape, René, 198
Paris Symphony, no. 31,
  K. 297, 44–45, 48–49,
  56–57
pedal piano, 110
Pellicia, Arrigo, 75
Perahia, Murray, 119,
  122–123, 125
Perlman, Itzhak, 66, 67, *67*

Persson, Miah, 187
Peters, Roberta, 197
Philarmonia Orchestra and
  Chorus, 180
Philips, 32, 75, 83, 122
piano
  fortepiano, 10, 110
  Mozart as pianist, 71
  pedal piano, 110
  See also piano concertos;
    piano music
piano concertos, 32, 183, 188
  Piano Concerto no. 5,
    K. 107 (Bach; arranged by
    Mozart), 126
  Piano Concerto no. 7,
    K. 242, 126
  Piano Concerto no. 10,
    K. 365, 126
  Piano Concerto no. 15,
    K. 450, 113, 129–130
  Piano Concerto no. 22,
    K. 482, 122
  Piano Concerto no. 23,
    K. 488, 121–122
  Piano Concerto no. 21 in
    C Major, K. 467, 109, 121,
    132–133
  Piano Concerto no. 25 in
    C Major, K. 503, 116–117,
    122, 131, 134
  Piano Concerto no. 24 in
    C Minor, K. 491, 113
  Piano Concerto no. 9 in
    E-flat Major, K. 271, 94,
    111–112, 127–128, 208
  See also concertos

piano music
  chamber music for, 125–126
  concertos, 108–117, 123–
    124, 126–135
  Mozart as pianist, 106–107
  for multiple pianos, 125–126
  recordings of, 117–123
  sonatas, 108–117, 123–124,
    135–137
  See also concertos; piano
    concertos; sonatas
Piano Quartets nos. 1 and 2, K.
  478 and K. 493, 83, 86
Piano Sonata no. 8, K. 310, 125
Piano Sonata no. 9, K. 311, 125
Pinnock, Travor, 43
Popp, Lucia, 197
posters
  Mostly Mozart 1978 (Nice),
    203
  Mostly Mozart 1984 (Bot-
    ero), 142
  Mostly Mozart 1974 (Bush),
    102
  Mostly Mozart 1995 (Baech-
    ler), *155*
  Mostly Mozart 1991 (Moth-
    erwell), *3*
Prague Chamber Orchestra, 32
Prague Symphony, no. 38, K.
  504, 21, 48, 59–60, 166
preludes, 137
Proust, Marcel, 202
Puchberg, Michael, 49, 90–91
Pushkin, Alexander, 14, 106

Quasthoff, Thomas, 198

Ramey, Samuel, 168
Rattle, Sir Simon, 186
Rauzzini, Matteo, 100
RCA, 75
recordings
    of chamber music, 82–83
    of concertante, 66–67
    of concertos, 75–76,
        117–123
    of *Haydn* Quartets, 82
    of operas, 152–153, 167–168,
        179–180, 186–187, 195–197
    of Requiem Mass in
        D Minor, K. 626, 98–99
    of sonatas, 117–123
    of symphonies and orchestral
        works, 43, 53–54
Regazzo, Lorenzo, 167
Rehak, Karel, 82
Remembrance of Things Past
    (Proust), 202
re pastore, Il (The Shepherd
    King), K. 208, 145
Requiem (Berlioz), 95
Requiem Mass in D Minor,
    K. 626, 33, 35, 88, 90,
    96–100, 103, 198
RIAS-Kammerchor, 197
Rice, Christine, 187
Rilling, Helmuth, 98–99
Rimsky-Korsakov, Nikolai, 14
Robles, Marisa, 75
Romantic period, 39
rondos
    about, 109, 127
    Rondo, K. 373, 75
    Rondo, K. 494, 137
    Rondo in D, K. 382, 138

Rorem, Ned, 172–173
Rosen, Charles, 202

Saint Matthew Passion (Bach), 89
Salieri, Antonio, 92, 198
    da Ponte and, 156
    Mozart symphonies con-
        ducted by, 38
    as portrayed in *Amadeus*
        (film), 14
    as portrayed in *Mozart and
        Salieri* (play), 106
Salzburg, 14–17, *15*
Salzburg Festival (1966), 167
Salzburg Festival (2006), 180
Schickele, Peter
    (P. D. Q. Bach), 51
Schiff, Andras, 119
Schikaneder, Emanuel, 188–190
Schrattenbach, Sigismund
    von, 15
Schubert, Franz, 31
Schwarz, Gerard, 67
Schwarzkopf, Elisabeth, 153,
    180, 187, 197
Scottish Chamber Orchestra,
    32, 153, 167, 187, 197
Scotto, Renata, 141
Second Symphony (Mahler), 95
Seiden, Cyndia, 152
Serenade in B-flat, K. 361. *See
    Gran Partita,* Serenade in
    B-flat, K. 361
Serenade in E-flat, 66
serenades, 65–66
Serkin, Peter, 80
Serkin, Rudolf, 80
Shaffer, Peter, 8

Shaw, George Bernard, 148–149
Sherman, Robert, 20
Siepi, Cesare, 180
Sills, Beverly, 196
Sinfonia Concertante, K. 364, 66, 69–70, 75
singspiel, 145–146
Solti, Sir Georg, 168, 186–187
sonatas, 108–117, 123–124, 135–137
    epistle sonatas, 101
    for multiple pianos, 125–126
    Piano Sonata no. 8, K. 310, 125
    Piano Sonata no. 9, K. 311, 125
    recordings of, 117–123
    sonata allegro form, 206
    Sonata in A Major, K. 331, 137
    Sonata in A Minor, K. 310, 128
    Sonata in C Major, K. 545, 117, 136–137
    Sonata in D Major, K. 448, 138
    Sonata in F Major, K. 533, 137
Sony, 82, 98
    Classical, 122–123, 125
    Legacy, 83
Spaethling, Robert, 21
Spencer, Stewart, 202
Steinberg, Michael, 37
Stern, Isaac, 83
Stoll, Anton, 101
String Quartet in B-flat, K. 465 *(The Hunt)*, 84
String Quartet in E-flat, K. 428, 82

String Quintets, K. 174, 406, 515, 516, 593, 614, 85–86
Süssmayr, Franz Xaver, 88, 98, 103
Sutherland, Joan, 180
Symphonierorchester des Bayerischen Rundfunks (Bavarian Radio Chorus and Orchestra), 99, 197
symphonies, 36–37, 127
    Haffner, no. 35, K. 385, 45–46, 57–58
    Jupiter, no. 41, K. 551, 37–38, 49–50, 50, 53, 61–62, 205–208
    Linz, no. 36, K. 425, 47–48, 58–59, 93
    Paris, no. 31, K. 297, 44–45, 48–49, 56–57
    Prague, no. 38, K. 504, 21, 48, 59–60, 166
    recordings of, 43, 53–54
    Symphony no. 39, K. 543, 37–38, 49–50, 60, 203
    Symphony no. 27 in G Major, K. 183, 42, 43, 55–56
    Symphony no. 40 in G Minor, 37–38, 49–50, 60–61
    unnamed, in G Major, K. 444 (M. Haydn), 47

Tallich Quartet, 82
Tate, Jeffrey, 32, 122
Taymor, Julie, 195
Telarc, 167, 187

Terfel, Bryn, 187
Theater auf der Wieden, 190, 198
Tian, Hao Jiang, 176–177

Uchida, Mitsuko, 80, 119, 122

Vaness, Carol, 167
variations, for piano, 137. *See also* piano music
Vespers, K. 339, 94–96, 100–101, 205
Vienna, 19–21, *24*
Vienna Philharmonic Orchestra, 54, 67, 99, 179–180, 186, 197
Violin Concertos nos. 1 through 5, K. 207, 211, 216, 218, 219, 76–77
vocal music, 87–93, 104–105
Ave verum corpus, K. 618, 95, 96–97, 101
Coronation Mass, K. 317, 89, 92
Exsultate jubilate in F Major, K. 165, 37, 94, 100
first cantata, K. 42, 102
Kyrie in D Minor, K. 341 (recording), 100
Masonic Cantata, K. 623, 97, 101–102
Mass in B Minor (Bach), 89

Mass in C Minor, K. 427, 90–91, 92–93, 100
Requiem Mass in D Minor, K. 626, 33, 35, 88, 90, 96–100, 103, 198
Vespers, K. 339, 94–96, 100–101, 101, 205
See also opera
von Karajan, Herbert, 53, 99
von Otter, Anne Sophie, 186
von Plankenstein, Baron, 156
von Stade, Frederica, 168

W.A. Mozart (Abert), 202
Walsegg-Stuppach, Count Franz von, 96
Walter, Anton, 109–110
Wand, Günter, 53
Weber, Aloysia, 17, 20, 150
Weber, Constanze. *See* Mozart, Constanze Weber (wife)
Women Are Like That. *See Così fan tutte* (Women Are Like That)
woodwinds, 52
Wunderlich, Fritz, 197

Zaide, K. 344, 145
Zauberflöte, Die. See Magic Flute, The
Zuckerman, Pinchas, 66, 67

9 781684 427031